FLYING SAUCERS—
HERE AND NOW!

BY FRANK EDWARDS

My First 10,000,000 Sponsors
Strangest of All
Stranger Than Science
Strange People
Strange World
Flying Saucers—Serious Business

By FRANK EDWARDS

Flying Saucers— Here and Now!

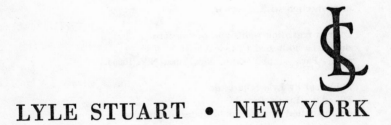

LYLE STUART • NEW YORK

To MARY, *my wife* . . .

This book is also respectfully dedicated to

MAJOR DONALD E. KEYHOE
U.S. MARINE CORPS, RETIRED

One of the first to sense the
truth in the field of UFOs, he
never lost heart and never took his
eye off the goal.
Thanks largely to his personal
sacrifices and dedicated efforts,
the moment of truth has been
brought closer.

Foreword

This is the chronicle of recorded events in the fascinating field of Unidentified Flying Objects in the past sixteen months. If the evidence constitutes what it seems to indicate, the presence of the UFOs amounts to one of the greatest news stories of all time and, as a professional newsman for more than forty years, I have tried to deal with it as such.

The worldwide nature of the riddle is clearly indicated by the worldwide origin of the mail that pours in on me these days. This is the direct result of my newspaper column, which is syndicated around the globe by Central Newsfeatures of London. My syndicated radio programs are distributed by Radiozark of Springfield, Missouri. My books are published by Lyle Stuart of New York City. And my lecture engagements are handled by Lordly and Dame, of Boston.

My especial thanks and gratitude are directed to Mrs. Idabel Epperson of Los Angeles, Mrs. V. Larsen of Seattle, Paul Cerny of San Francisco, C. W. Fitch of Cleveland, Richard Hall and the staff at NICAP and John P. Bessor of Pittsburgh. I also wish to thank the many editors of the newspapers which carry my column around the world and their newsmen and the scholars among their readers for the innumerable contributions they have made. And I am grateful indeed to those individuals who wish to remain anonymous, due to their official connections with their respective governments, for their important assistance in the compilation of the growing record of this remarkable development.

To those who are interested in the factual evidence in the field of Unidentified Flying Objects, I recommend that they join NICAP, the world's largest civilian organization dealing with this problem, headed by an imposing array of hundreds of scientists and retired military leaders. Membership is $5 per year; the address is: 1536 Connecticut Avenue, N.W., Washington, D.C.

The opinions expressed herein are, unless otherwise specifically accredited, solely those of the author, and do not necessarily represent the views or opinions of any organization or individuals living or dead, in this world or in transit between the planets.

Sincerely—
Frank Edwards

Indianapolis
June, 1967.

FLYING SAUCERS—
HERE AND NOW!

"I assure you, Madam, if any such creatures as you describe really existed, we would be the first to know about it."

1

In 1966 and 1967—

Two UFOs cross the face of the sun—and startled astronomers at a famous observatory photograph one of them.

A jetliner carrying some executives of a major plane manufacturer finds itself paced by a UFO for seven minutes—in broad daylight.

Two American astronauts in orbit excitedly radio down descriptions of two strange objects that seem to be pacing their craft—only to have their report cut off at the Space Center.

Australian authorities confirm the nature of strange "saucer nests" in several lagoons, where the UFOs are estimated to have weighed thirty tons.

A British housewife's movies of UFOs are dismissed with a phoney "explanation" by authorities.

Hundreds of police watch strange lighted objects maneuvering at low altitude over midwestern communities.

A pilot observes a UFO, which is being tracked simultaneously on radar.

Scientists speak out—demand scientific investigations of Unidentified Flying Objects as a major problem.

A Soviet scientist says UFOs are based on Mars and that Russia has had the same problems with them that the USA has experienced.

Those are just a few of the many interesting developments in this fascinating field in the past year.

It led one scientist, an authority on UFOs, to say:

"These unidentified flying objects are not a military problem, but they do constitute a scientific problem and should be dealt with as such."

The gentleman who made that statement has been, since 1948, the top scientific consultant to the Air Force on the subject of UFOs, Dr. J. Allen Hynek, astronomer at Northwestern University.

He was one of those who recommended to the House Military Affairs Committee a policy identical to that which the National Investigations Committee on Aerial Phenomena had been urging for years. That organization, popularly known as NICAP, is headed by admirals and generals and scientists in many fields. It has long sought a Congressional probe of the manner in which information regarding UFOs has been suppressed by the United States government, acting through the Air Force. NICAP's distinguished board had long ago taken the position that the UFOs were not a military problem, but a scientific problem of global nature, and should be dealt with on that basis.

And now, after years of frustrating rebuffs, we found the top Air Force scientist advocating exactly what so many of us had tried, and failed, to achieve.

Dr. Hynek's surprising statement was just one of the many surprising turns taken by UFO developments during 1966. It was a year that saw the subject suddenly become respectable again. Major magazines dredged up just about anything they could find to feature on the subject. Book publishers, eager to get in on the demand for books on UFOs, went back as far as the early 1950's for material to reprint. Retitled and with different covers, they offered it

14

to a public that had long forgotten such characters as George Adamski. One major national magazine even featured a story by a couple who told the latest version of the contactee yarns—which we will examine later. But the most important aspect of the Year of Surprises was the treatment accorded to UFO news and sightings by the press of the nation.

By early 1966 the Unidentified Flying Objects were front-page news again. And there they remained for the balance of the year. They shared the front page with the more prosaic accounts of wars and floods and murders and, in so doing, they once again became subject matter for conversation among respected citizens; for the evidence of their existence had become so overwhelming that they could no longer be denied.

This upsurge in prominence for the UFOs in 1966 was the direct outgrowth of their dramatic mass appearances in 1965, culminating in the night of August 2-3, when an estimated quarter of a million persons stood out in the Great Plains states of the United States and watched the formations of unusual lights maneuvering overhead.

The things were seen with the naked eye and with a wide variety of optical instruments. They were tracked on radar, both civilian and military. They were photographed by both amateur and professional photographers. They followed planes, including a jet passenger plane piloted by a good friend of mine.

Next morning when the official explanation was handed out, assuring one and all that they had seen nothing more than four stars in the constellation Orion, my pilot friend commented wryly:

"Last night was the first time in my life that I have flown across Nebraska with three stars under my right wing!"

Professional astronomers quickly pointed out that the official explanation explained nothing, since the constellation Orion was, at that time, visible only from the other side of Earth!

The Air Force announced that it would continue to investigate—but the damage had been done. The news media finally realized that they had been hoodwinked by these official explanations for years—and they didn't like it. A rash of angry editorials denouncing the official policy of concealment and deception and demanding the facts made print immediately following the ill-starred (no pun intended) faux pas of August 3, 1965.

That unlikely explanation brought into focus a problem with which the Air Force had been struggling for years—the dilemma of how to explain something as nothing. It was a duty to which the Air Force had been assigned by official order. It was an assignment which they had tried to carry out to the best of their ability under the severe restrictions imposed by the regulation.

Students of the UFO problem—civilian students—interpreted the mass appearance of the objects in 1965 as part of an anticipated program. It seemed to be the sixth phase of a seven-phase program which our military had foreseen as far back as the early 1950s: the appearance of the objects to the greatest number of people in order to demonstrate their presence—and their lack of hostility. If this estimate was the correct one, then they should be making more landings and close-in approaches in the months ahead—and our own approach to the subject of UFOs could—and should—be changed.

Have either or both of these developments occurred?

Let's examine the record.

"Never mind the five o'clock traffic report . . . here's a special news bulletin!"

Drawn for BROADCASTING by Sid Hix

2

The New Jersey State Police radio station at Pompton Lakes flashed the alert to its personnel—and to the officers who served as reservoir guards at Wanaque impoundment—that an unidentified flying object was moving toward the reservoir.

Within a matter of minutes Mayor Harry Wolfe of Wanaque, accompanied by his son and two city policemen, Arthur Barton and Warren Hagstrom, were on the scene at the dam. They watched a glowing object which maneuvered at very low altitude over the frozen reservoir, as did the guards, George Dykman and George Destito. Before it left the scene, the witnesses said that the object had sent down beams of light which apparently melted holes in the ice on the reservoir.

That incident occurred on the night of January 11, 1966. The year was getting off to a running start.

At 2 a.m. on the morning of January 12, two city police officers of Wanaque radioed to headquarters that the "thing" was back over the reservoir again, darting erratically from place to place, and that they were watching it through binoculars. As it had done in its earlier visit, the UFO sent down a few bolts of bright light, then streaked away and vanished in the night.

Although this bizarre event took place in full view of many credible witnesses, within thirty miles of Times

Square in New York City, it was virtually unknown across the nation until publication of my book, *Flying Saucers— Serious Business.*

I mention this particular incident at this point in our discussion because it was due for a re-run—as they say on television—in 1966.

October 16, 1966, to be precise.

Hundreds of spectators, including Mayor Harry Wolfe of Wanaque, lined the banks of the reservoir to watch a glowing reddish object which reportedly zigzagged around overhead.

Said the Mayor: "I saw the object. It was hovering over the reservoir. It was red in color and it was zigzagging all over the place. It was the size of an automobile."

At Pompton Lakes, the police radio switchboard was reportedly swamped with calls from persons who wanted to report that they were watching—or had been watching— the same or a similar object. Reservoir police reported that hundreds of persons were tramping along the banks of the reservoir hoping for a glimpse of the thing.

Said the dispatcher for the police radio at Pompton Lakes: "Cars are parked bumper to bumper all around the lake. If you don't get there early you don't get a place!"

The reason for this unusual interest in parking space around Wanaque Reservoir in New Jersey stemmed from the fact that on the preceding Monday night, October 10th, many residents of the area, plus four police officers, had spotted the UFO in and around the reservoir which had been the scene of the visitation of the previous January.

On the first appearance of the UFO, in January of 1966, the Air Force at Stewart Air Force Base had blandly assured the news media that the object seen at Wanaque Reservoir was nothing more than "a special helicopter

20

with a bright light on it." This explanation was subsequently retracted when curious newsmen indicated that they were unwilling to accept the statement. The Air Force spokesman admitted that there had been no helicopter in that area at that time.

Now, in October of 1966, when the same credible witnesses were seeing a similar object over the same body of water, they did not bother to report it to the Air Force. They told newsmen that since they had been ridiculed by the Air Force investigating team which conducted a probe of the January sighting they had no intention of subjecting themselves to the same treatment in connection with the October sightings.

And the Air Force officials assigned to Project Blue Book, the government's UFO investigative agency, told the *Morning Call* of Paterson, New Jersey, that it would not investigate the sighting until someone filed a report— which nobody cared to file, evidently.

As a matter of fact, Blue Book was virtually at a standstill by the time the UFO came back to Wanaque in October of 1966. The Air Force was not looking for any new cases to explain. It was merely biding its time. Many things had happened in the field of the Unidentified Flying Objects and at least one of them had taught the Air Force a painful and rather humiliating lesson.

The catastrophic "explanation" of August 3, 1965, which had backfired so promptly on the Air Force, had admittedly weakened its position as a credible source of UFO statements. The incident which completely deflated the Air Force with regard to UFO explanations grew out of a complex of incidents in and near Ann Arbor, Michigan.

It all began on Sunday night, March 20, 1966.

Frank Mannors, 47, was a truck driver who lived at

10600 McGuiness. His home is surrounded by open farm land, the conventional open fields and rolling country common to that part of Michigan.

Mannors said that when he stepped outside about 8:00 p.m. he first noticed the thing. At first he thought it was a "falling star"—a brightly lighted object that was plunging swiftly and silently to Earth. Then, all of a sudden, this thing stopped. Just above the top of the trees it came to an abrupt halt and Mannors said that he could see that it carried red and blue lights, with a white light which seemed to be rotating.

According to the account he later gave to the authorities, Mannors yelled for his wife and the rest of the family to come out quickly. In addition to Mrs. Mannors, their 19-year-old son Ronald and their daughter and her husband all rushed out in response to Mr. Mannors' excited call.

Their descriptions all tallied.

"You could see it rise from the ground and hit the tree-tops awhile and then fall back to the ground. It would turn different colors—white when it was on the ground and blue and red in the treetops and then it would come down and change back to white again."

Mannors ran inside and called the Dexter police.

By the time he got outside again the object was making another of its slow climbs to treetop height—then it slowly sank back to Earth. Mannors and his son decided to go take a close look at the thing, whatever it was.

"We got to within five hundred yards of that thing and we could see the shape of it," Mannors told Police Chief Robert Taylor and Officer N. G. Lee, who had responded to Mannors' call for help. "This thing had a light here and a light there and a white light that looked like we were looking at some kind of a porthole or something. It wasn't saucer shaped. It was more like pyramid shaped and it had a coral surface."

He indicated to the police that the lights on the object were on the ends of the thing. Both Mannors and his son estimated that the object was about the length of an ordinary automobile. Both agreed that it had a quilted surface. Beneath it, they said, something appeared to be turning. They were able to see details because of the light given off by the object, they told police.

What happened next?

The lights had gone out on the object by the time Mannors and his boy could reach the scene, but both men saw a strange light settle down about half a mile away.

Others saw that same light—including the two police officers who were on their way to answer Mannors' call.

Chief Taylor said: "We could see that light from the hill. It looked like it was down in the swamp—just a red glow. With binoculars we could see it easily, pulsating with a red light."

His fellow officer confirmed the appearance of the light.

By this time the two Dexter police officers had been joined by Washtenaw County Deputies Stanley McFadden and David Fitzpatrick. Still another Dexter policeman, Robert Hunawill, arrived at about this same time.

The officers later reported that, as they attempted to close in on the thing in the swamp, it vanished. Its red glow disappeared as the police flashlights probed for it. Then the officers heard a roar, like a siren or the turning of heavy machinery at great speed. Chief Taylor and his companions saw a red object streaking away toward Mannors' house at high velocity. Patrolman Hunawill, who was in the patrol car, reported seeing a strange object bearing red and white lights. He estimated that it was about a thousand feet high when it came into his view. He told Air Force officials that it made several sweeps over the swamp before it was joined by three similar objects and the formation moved away and vanished in the night.

Mannors and his son had returned to their home. The whole family assertedly heard a high-pitched whine "like the ricochet of a bullet" as the object passed over the house.

Around the area, other officers were becoming witnesses to some strange sights. While her husband and son were making their approach to the lighted thing in the swamp, Mrs. Mannors had called the Sheriff's office to report that a thing which seemed to be a flying saucer was down near her home. The two Deputies previously mentioned were first on the scene—others followed. In all, six patrol cars and three detectives were rushed to the area.

Deputy Fitzpatrick said that as he and another officer made their way into the swamp they saw a brilliant light. When they got back to their car they were informed by a Dexter police officer (Hunawill) that an object with flashing red and green lights, moving close to Earth, had hovered briefly above the Deputies' car before zooming up to join three similar objects moving across the area.

Under questioning by police officers at the time, Mannors and his boy agreed that the thing they had seen was ". . . the length of an ordinary automobile . . . sort of football-shaped . . . kind of yellowish-gray in color and it had a surface that was pitted [or quilted]. It seemed to be sitting about eight feet above the ground . . . on a kind of fog or steam. The lights on it . . . green on one end and white on the other . . . were pulsating and each light had a halo around it."

Then, said the witnesses, the object slowly turned a deep red all over—like molten iron—and when the Mannors boy exclaimed, "Look at that horrible thing!" all the lights suddenly went out and they did not see it again until it was airborne.

The police took down Mannors' story, made notes of their own observations and experiences, and went back to Dexter to compare accounts.

There were a couple of additional chapters on which the authorities had not counted.

The 16-year-old son of the Police Chief, Robert Taylor, reported that at 10:30 p.m. he had watched a strange object in the sky, flashing red and white lights. Young Taylor said he watched it moving eastward for a couple of minutes and then it abruptly changed course and sped away westward.

Also to be heard from was another Deputy Sheriff, in this case Deputy Ford Bushroe. He reported that at 11:15, as he and his fellow officer were heading back into Ann Arbor after having taken part in the investigation of the Mannors incident, they noticed a brilliant bluish-green object carrying red and white lights. Both officers said the thing appeared to be domed . . . or at least it had some sort of rounded superstructure.

Deputy Sheriff Bushroe says in his report:

> "We were doing about seventy miles an hour and we couldn't keep up with it. It stayed ahead of us easily. It was about fifteen hundred feet above the ground and must have been going around a hundred miles an hour. It was headed west. We stopped chasing it when we lost it behind some trees."

Next day detectives searched the spot where the object had apparently touched down . . . or hovered at a few feet above ground . . . but they could find no real evidence. Even the Geiger counters revealed no indication of any unusual radioactivity.

(Just for the record, the Chrysler space agency complex, near Dexter, and the eighty-five foot University of Michigan radio telescope a few miles from Mannors' home, both were inactive on the Sunday night of these events.)

Authorities at nearby Selfridge Field, instead of investigating the sighting reports themselves, as is customary for the nearest Air Force base, had passed the case on to Washington, D.C., for consideration and further action, if any.

On Monday night, March 21st, there was ample commotion in and around the scene of the previous night's action.

The road to Frank Mannors' home was jammed with cars occupied by the curious and the kooks. One character turned his spotlight straight upward and blinked it for about an hour in a pattern which he said was part of a mathematical formula which the operators of the UFOs would certainly recognize. If they did, they gave no indication of it. Another lad played his fiddle in a futile attempt to lure the UFOs within range. His efforts at least got his picture in the papers. Still other daffies devoted their time to heckling the Mannors by smart alec phone calls, by throwing rocks and bottles at their house, and by other equally ingenious procedures conjured up by such meager mentalities.

The crowd of curious who jammed the road near Frank Mannors' farm home had missed the action by about seventy-five miles. On that remarkable Monday night it was taking place near Hillsdale College, at Hillsdale, Michigan.

Starting during a thunderstorm about 10 p.m. and continuing until a little after 2 a.m. next morning, some of the faculty members and at least eighty-seven of the coeds at the college watched a fascinating display of lights in a swamp not far from the campus. Among those who witnessed this spectacle were several local police, the security police at the college, and the Hillsdale County Civil Defense Director, William Van Horn.

Some of the witnesses got much better opportunities to observe details in the objects than others, who were at a greater distance from the objects. Those who were nearest all agreed that the things had definite form, which they described as football-shaped. They also agreed that the objects carried bright lights fore and aft; that these lights flashed red and blue-green and that the objects were controlled craft of some sort, traveling in a formation which they changed from time to time.

From the windows of the dormitories at the college, scores of witnesses—including some of the faculty members at the school—observed the antics of these weird lighted craft. A few of the girls had binoculars and a few others had opera glasses, through which they were able to improve the viewing conditions.

These sightings at Hillsdale College, coming right on the heels of the incident on Frank Mannors' farm and its attendant developments in that same general area, made headlines across the nation. The Air Force was in a squeeze —it had to come up with some kind of answer to offset this widespread publicity.

On Tuesday, March 22, 1966, the Air Force announced that it was going to call in its top scientific advisor, Dr. J. Allen Hynek, to solve the riddle of the much-discussed sightings at Dexter and Hillsdale, Michigan.

Dr. Hynek came, and saw, and explained.

27

He presented his findings on the matter at the Detroit Press Club on Friday, March 25th, to a packed house.

Dr. Hynek brushed off the sightings in and around Hillsdale College as the work of pranksters playing with flares. (How they got the flares to fly in formation and to change places in formation was not revealed.)

Referring to a photograph made by a police officer at Milan, Michigan (see picture section), Dr. Hynek dismissed that as "nothing more than a time exposure of the rising moon and the planet Venus." (How these objects traveled so far across the sky in twenty seconds was not explained.)

Then he got down to the meat in the coconut—to the Dexter case.

Said Dr. Hynek: "The majority of observers in both cases have reported only lights—red, yellow and green; silent lights glowing near the ground." (Four of the police officers and the Mannors family also reported sounds as the object took off.—F.E.)

Continuing, Dr. Hynek noted that the only two witnesses who had been close enough to the scene to describe an object were admittedly five hundred yards—a quarter of a mile—distant. Too far, he noted, for anyone to determine the details.

In both the case of the Mannors family and that of the police officers who observed the glowing red object on the ground, Dr. Hynek said that the witnesses had seen the object or the light in a swamp, and he added:

"A dismal swamp is a most unlikely place for visitors from outer space! It is not the place where a helicopter would hover for several hours, or where a soundless secret device would be likely to be tested."

To say that a swamp is a most unlikely place for a space ship to land is to overlook the fact that our own space program has for years included just such a provision. If one of our spacecraft reaches a planet that is inhabited—and if that craft needs examination or adjustment—it will endeavor to land in a desert or swamp, where it would presumably have the best chance for freedom from interference by the inhabitants of that planet. Dr. Hynek's contention that such a landing on our own planet is unlikely is at variance with logic.

Then Dr. Hynek dropped the other shoe.

He told his news audience that a likely explanation of the phenomena which had been witnessed by all those people in Dexter and Hillsdale was nothing more than "swamp gas," sometimes called "fox fire" or "will o' the wisp." And he explained that swamp gas is due to rotting vegetation which produces a gas that ignites on contact with the oxygen in the air.

"Swamp gas" was such a preposterous explanation that it promptly became standard joke material. Cartoonists had a field day with it. Editorial writers seized upon it to flay the Air Force again for its apparent policy of deception and concealment. Dr. Hynek, having issued the statement, became the butt of the jokes, and he didn't like it.

Writing in the *Saturday Evening Post* for December 17, 1966, Dr. Hynek says that in the midst of his efforts to investigate the sightings at Dexter and Hillsdale he was notified by the Air Force that he would hold a press conference and he would issue a statement of "explanation"—although he says that he had no idea what had caused the sightings.

Dr. Hynek says that when he handed out the statement which discussed swamp gas, he was horrified to see a newsman underline the word and rush for a telephone. The "possible" answer was seized upon as Dr. Hynek's solution

29

and the fat was in the fire, both for him and for the Air Force.

In connection with this incident I should like to report that Dr. Hynek did not want to offer the "swamp gas" explanation but that he was virtually forced into it. As an employee of the Air Force—since 1948 he has been their top scientific advisor on UFOs—Dr. Hynek has to do what he is told to do by the Air Force—and this case in Michigan seems to have been such an example. I am told by a fellow newsman who was there that Dr. Hynek and the Air Force representatives had a heated argument about the advisability of issuing the swamp gas statement and that Hynek apparently was finally *ordered* to do it—with results which have certainly vindicated his reported opposition to it.

With the "swamp gas" explanation following on the heels of its fiasco of August 3, 1965, the Air Force hit bottom. As a credible source of explanations for UFOs, Project Blue Book was at its lowest ebb.

The accuracy of this observation was emphasized by the experience of a major aircraft industry official who contacted the Air Force in late 1966 to request that some Air Force official talk to his club about Unidentified Flying Objects. After a bit of hemming and hawing, the Air Force official spokesman said: "Well, to be quite honest with you, since our 'swamp gas' explanation in Michigan last spring we don't send our men out on these speechmaking trips any more. It gets too embarrassing for them when that matter is brought up!"

In telling me of this interesting talk, the official of the company added: "They won't be able to tell me these things aren't real! A couple of months ago several of the Vice Presidents of the company were on a flight to Wichita in a company plane. In broad daylight the pilot told us to look out the left windows quickly. We looked. And out there a few hundred feet off our wingtip was a UFO sailing serenely along. It flew out there for several minutes and it changed a lot of minds, including my own!"

Just for the record, he was one of the Vice Presidents of Boeing Aircraft, world's largest maker of commercial planes.

"Why bother to phone? They'll just say it's swamp gas."

3

The reaction to the "swamp gas" explanation was fast and furious.

One of the first to go on record was the *South Bend* (Indiana) *Tribune*, which said editorially:

"AIR FORCE INSULTS PUBLIC WITH SWAMP-GAS THEORY

"We have always stood in the front rank of skeptics when it came to swallowing unidentified-flying-object reports.

"But we must admit that some of the official Air Force investigator's explanations of recent sightings seem almost as far fetched as the 'little green men' approaches.

"The recent official conclusion that a series of Michigan UFO sightings could be explained as 'swamp gas' was strained, to say the least.

". . . Those of us who can shrug off the unexplained sightings as unworthy of staying awake at night about prefer not to have our common sense insulted by far-fetched 'official' theories, either."

The *Richmond* (Virginia) *News Leader* said on March 23, "It is high time for the Air Force to cease suppressing any hard evidence relating to such phenomena" and called upon it to discontinue its policy of attempting "to discredit the testimony of witnesses."

The *Dallas Morning News* commented (March 30) that "a serious UFO investigation might earn great dividends for this nation."

The *Cincinnati Enquirer* said on April 2: "If there is any substantial evidence that any of the sightings can be attributed to objects either intra- or interplanetary the Air Force should reveal it to us. It is man's nature to be curious about that which goes on about him. It is also man's nature to fear the unknown."

Scores of newspapers editorially called for a full and open disclosure of what was known about the UFOs and for an end to the obvious policy of deception and deliberate misstatements from official sources.

Not all newspapers called for open dealing with the public, however. The *New York Times* brushed off the whole subject as beneath its dignity. The *Chicago Tribune* alleged that UFOs were in the same category with such frivolities as "water fights and panty raids." Which leads me to believe that the *Chicago Tribune* hasn't learned much since it announced that Thomas E. Dewey had been elected President.

A careful look at that swamp gas explanation seems to indicate that the Air Force was desperate for something to say. Already on the ropes for their gaffe of August 3 of the previous year and, with scores of highly credible witnesses involved in the sightings at Dexter and Hillsdale, Michigan, they seem to have seized upon another ill-chosen hypothesis as about the best they could think of in the circumstances.

Dr. Hynek has said since that memorable Detroit press conference that he offered the swamp gas explanation as nothing more than a *possible* explanation. This is quite likely correct but, since it was the *only* suggested solution offered, it automatically acquired the status of the definitive solution.

The critical weakness in the swamp gas hypothesis was

that the Air Force was simply offering a theory as the answer to a riddle. Since nobody has ever caught, or cut, or weighed a so-called "will o' the wisp," then scientifically it remains purely conjectural—a convenient hypothesis for use in such cases as the one under discussion.

It is true that we know what marsh gases are: It is not true that we know what "will o' the wisps" are.

Scientific reaction to the proffered swamp gas solution came quickly.

John F. Sullivan, a chemical engineer of twenty-three years' experience, told the *Royal Oak* (Michigan) *Tribune* on March 26th: "Methane [swamp gas] will not rise high into the air, nor will it hover and fly away at high speeds. It would at most burn only for a few minutes. It would have the appearance of a torch [flashlight] . . . nobody could mistake it for a fire." Sullivan added that Dr. Hynek's use of this hypothesis indicated to him that either Dr. Hynek knew little about marsh gas, he was not telling the truth, or his credentials were no good.

On the NBC "Tonight" show, shortly after the incidents at Dexter and Hillsdale, Johnny Carson was questioning Dr. Albert Hibbs, a scientist from the California Institute of Technology. Carson asked Dr. Hibbs if he accepted the swamp gas theory as a valid explanation for the Michigan sightings. Dr. Hibbs replied that he did not. "The characteristics of marsh gas are not in accord with what was reported there."

The *NICAP Investigator,* a publication issued regularly to its members by NICAP, dealt with this issue by quoting from M. Minnaert's work on *The Nature of Light and Colour in the Open Air.* Minnaert says that swamp or marsh gas consists of combustible methane, carbon dioxide, and nitrogen resulting from decaying vegetable matter in marshy areas. Of the lights produced by these gases, he says: "Sometimes they resemble tiny flames, about ½ to 5 inches long and not more than 2 inches broad. Sometimes they are right on the ground, at other times they float about 4 inches above it. That they dance about is apparently not true . . . occasionally they are blown along by the wind for a few feet before they are extinguished."

Stuck with an explanation that was both editorially and scientifically unacceptable, the Air Force soon found itself on the receiving end in still another sense.

Several newspapers took up the issue by advocating a full-scale Congressional investigation of the whole puzzling business: the nature of the UFOs, the manner in which the investigations of them had been conducted, and the manner in which the public had been dealt with both during and after the various investigations.

This procedure, which NICAP had been advocating for years, was already in the works by the time most of the news media took up the hue and cry. Congressman Gerald Ford of Michigan, Minority Leader in the House, had already held press conferences and made television appearances demanding that Congress investigate the very strange antics which devolved around the Air Force handling of UFO cases.

At first it seemed that there would be a full-scale probe of the matter. But it dwindled to a one-day event . . . a hearing before the House Armed Services Committee on April 5, 1966. Although it brought out some interesting admissions, it was, by and large, a flanking movement by the Air Force which got them around the problem of a full-scale probe by going through the motions of a lesser investigation. By holding it at the height of the clamor, it brought about a subsidence of the denunciatory reaction in the press without actually forcing the Pentagon to yield any of its prerogatives.

Playing to a jampacked audience, the hearing got widespread publicity.

Chairman Mendel Rivers read into the record a letter from Congressman Gerald Ford, protesting the swamp gas answer in the Michigan sightings, stating that the American people are entitled to better explanations, and naming a retired Air Force Colonel who had seen a UFO and was willing to testify before the committee about it. He also placed in the record a syndicated newspaper article by columnist Roscoe Drummond, citing NICAP evidence and urging "a more detached and credible appraisal of evidence." Then Rivers placed in the record six newspaper articles by veteran Capitol newsman Bulkley Griffin, who after lengthy investigation asserted that the Air Force was withholding facts from the public while at the same time it was publishing incorrect explanations.

Having inserted this amount of material in opposition to the Pentagon policy on UFOs, Chairman Rivers then added an item which consisted of a letter from Colonel D. W. Covell, Congressional Inquiry Division of the Air Force, in which Covell denied that there ever had been a Top Secret conclusion that the UFOs were interplanetary. (The existence of the conclusion had been confirmed to NICAP by Captain Edward J. Ruppelt, former chief of Project Blue Book, and by Colonel Dewey Fourney, former Air Force Intelligence Major and monitor of the Air Force UFO project.)

Continuing, Congressman Rivers also added to the hearing record an article from *Life* magazine which quoted Major Hector Quintanilla, Jr., head of the Air Force UFO explanation division at Dayton, as saying that it was impossible to prove that the UFOs are nonexistent, and adding that the Air Force would not give up chasing them.

"Just imagine," Quintanilla was quoted as saying, "what a great thing it would be to get our hands on a ship from another planet and to examine its power plant."

During the course of the hearing, Congressman Richard S. Schweiker of Pennsylvania asked Major Quintanilla if it were true that none of the unexplained objects have been sighted on radar.

Major Quintanilla did not answer the question directly. Instead he replied: "We have no radar cases which are unexplained."

(As a matter of fact a great many radar and visual-radar sightings of record are not explained. Perhaps the witness was playing on words: He may have been taking the position that if the object was listed as a UFO then it had been identified!)

Congressman Schweiker then drew from Quintanilla the admission that he had received a report on the famed Exeter, New Hampshire, sighting from two officers at Pease Air Force Base, who had investigated the case.

"What were their conclusions?" Schweiker asked.

"They couldn't explain it," Major Quintanilla replied.

It might be noted here that this Air Force spokesman on UFOs left the two investigating officers from Pease Air Force Base holding the bag on the Exeter case. Major Quintanilla failed to mention the part he had played in the case, by assuring the news media that the police and other witnesses at Exeter had been "misled" by low-flying flights of Air Force planes, including a refueling operation.

After the case had been widely publicized in the *NICAP Investigator, Look* magazine, and elsewhere, Major Quintanilla went back and requestioned two of the police officers who had been witnesses to the "oval-shaped object 80-90 feet long, carrying blinking brilliant red lights, which at times hovered within a hundred feet of the ground."

The officers were Eugene Bertrand and David Hunt, both of the Exeter police force and both with fine records. Bertrand is a former Air Force crewman and is well versed in refueling flights. Both officers told Major Quintanilla they resented his implication that they did not recognize conventional planes and that they resented the press release which had held them up to ridicule. The Major returned to his headquarters and sent the two officers a letter in which he withdrew the hasty "explanation" . . . but he did *not* withdraw it in a public statement. Nor did he mention this maneuver when questioned about that case before the House Armed Services Committee.

This was an instance where the House Armed Services Committee could have used advantageously the services of someone who knew the background of the subject before the Committee. As in all such cases, the inquiry can be no better than the questions that are asked. If the witnesses know the subject more intimately than the interrogators, then the witnesses are running the show. And to a large extent that seems to have been the case with the UFO hearings in the spring of 1966.

In addition to the performance given by Major Quintanilla, there was an interesting session with Air Force Secretary Harold Brown, when Congressman Rivers observed: "We can't just write them [UFOs] off. There are too many responsible people who are concerned."

Secretary Brown replied by reading a prepared statement. It was double-barreled; the first half was right out of the standard Air Force statistical sheets, issued each time the UFOs get the heat on the Air Force. The other half—the last half—is self explanatory.

Secretary Brown's prepared statement declared that UFOs posed no threat, were not extraterrestrial, and were more than 90 percent explained. This much was standard stuffing. Then he introduced a memorandum from the Director of Information, Major General E. B. LeBailly. The memorandum said, "Many of the reports that cannot be explained have come from intelligent and technically well qualified individuals whose integrity cannot be questioned." LeBailly asked for a scientific panel to review Project Blue Book.

Chairman Rivers then asked Secretary Brown if anyone in authority had alleged that UFOs might come from other planets.

Secretary Brown replied that no one in the Air Force had said this—as far as he knew. Here again the Committee was sorely in need of informed support. They could have told the Committee, and got it into the hearing records, that Colonel J. J. Bryan, III, USAF Retired, and former aviation advisor to NATO, had stated his conclusions on the interplanetary nature of UFOs—as have Lieutenant Colonel Howard Strand, a base commander in the Air National Guard, and many others, *both in and out of the Air Force.*

Colonel Bryan (now a member of the NICAP Board of Governors) says in a letter to Major Donald E. Keyhoe, Director of NICAP:

"I am aware that hundreds of military and airline pilots, airport personnel, astronomers, missile trackers and other competent observers have reported sightings of Unidentified Flying Objects. I am also aware that many of these

UFOs have been observed maneuvering in formation, and that many were simultaneously being tracked by radar. It is my opinion that:

"The UFOs reported by competent observers are devices under intelligent control.

"Their speeds, maneuvers and other technical evidence prove them superior to any aircraft or space devices now produced on earth.

"These UFOs are interplanetary devices systematically observing the earth, either manned or under remote control, or both.

"Information on UFOs, including sightings reports, has been and is still being officially withheld. This policy is dangerous, especially since mistaken identification of UFOs as a secret Russian attack might accidentally set off war. Unless the policy is changed, a Congressional investigation should be held to reduce or eliminate this and other dangers."

This, from a former Special Assistant to the Secretary of the Air Force (1952-1953); and later assigned as an aviation advisor on the staff of General Lauris Norstad, then head of NATO. He wears the Air Medal with two gold stars.

The Secretary of the Air Force, during his session on the witness stand at this House Armed Services Committee hearing, managed to insert into the hearing record that the Air Force was not withholding any information on UFOs from the public; that there was no evidence that UFOs were real objects and that no witnesses were being subjected to ridicule. It was just more of the same, and perhaps—under the restrictions imposed by regulations—all that he *could* say.

One of the most interesting, and in some ways informative, portions of the hearing was that devoted to Dr. J. Allen Hynek, for eighteen years the top scientific advisor to the Air Force in the field of UFO research.

Dr. Hynek admitted that during the past twenty years the public concern and interest in UFOs had grown steadily, in spite of what he called "the seeming silliness" of the whole business. Then he added that in the past many matters of great value to science had been overlooked because the new phenomenon simply did not fit the accepted scientific outlook. In this connection he noted that while the working hypothesis of the Air Force—that all UFO reports added up to nothing—had been successful (from the Air Force standpoint) it might add up to a roadblock to research that would be meaningful, for, he said "if one digs too intently for coal he is apt to miss diamonds."

Under questioning, Hynek admitted that he had warned the Air Force that Project Blue Book was not fully investigating some UFO cases . . . cases in which the witnesses were of such caliber that their reports warranted something better than the offhand treatment accorded by the boys at Blue Book . . . and treatment actually beyond that which Project Blue Book was capable of delivering.

Congressman Lucien Nedzi of Michigan then asked Dr. Hynek:

"Has there ever been any evidence in any of these unexplained sightings that would indicate that there is some kind of extraterrestrial intelligence involved?"

Hynek replied cautiously:

"I have never seen any evidence to confirm this . . . however, the possibility should be kept open as a possible hypothesis. I don't think we should ever close our minds to it."

In one day the House Armed Services Committee had

endeavored to deal with a problem of twenty years' growth. In one day the Congressmen had sought to thresh out the accumulation of two decades of contradiction and controversy—of charge and counter-charge. That they barely scratched the surface was not surprising. That they even made the gesture is the part that *is* surprising.

But if we are to be realistic about such things, we must take into consideration the conditions under which a member of Congress, or a committee of Congress, must operate when moving against the wishes or policies of the Defense Department.

Let us be mindful of the manner in which so-called "defense contracts" or "space contracts" are carefully parceled out around the country. Committee Chairmen are generously dealt with in the awarding of these choice industrial plums. An excellent example was the case of the late Senator Harry Byrd of Virginia: Each time he would make a statement that he was planning to reduce the military budget that statement was duly published. And time after time the military would find some choice shipbuilding contracts for the shipyards in the Senator's home state, and his zeal for cutting the budget would diminish accordingly.

With so many hundreds of these contracts scattered around the land, just about every member of Congress is receptive to keeping in the good graces of the Defense Department. It would be unrealistic of us to expect very many Congressmen to probe too deeply into any Pentagon policy that might be embarrassing to the Defense Department, including that of withholding evidence about UFOs.

This, in my opinion, explains why there was no investigation of the UFO matter by Congress in 1961, although NICAP was repeatedly promised that it would be done.

And this relationship between Congress and the military may explain the manner in which the UFO hearings of April 1, 1966, were conducted—having the form, but not the substance, of a really penetrating and meaningful probe of the issue at hand.

Perhaps the most far reaching single statement to emanate from that entire hearing is the one quoted at the beginning of this book, Dr. Hynek's statement that the UFOs were not a military problem but a scientific problem —and that they should be dealt with as such.

For it was from this hearing that there developed the plan of hiring a group of civilian scientists at a major university to investigate some of the sightings.

In the course of time, this led to a contract for $313,000 between the government and the University of Colorado, where a group of scientists under Dr. Edward U. Condon agreed to accept the assignment.

The Air Force stated publicly that Dr. Condon's group would be encouraged to operate independently and would be permitted to make its findings public, even though they might be at variance with the established Air Force position. In addition to Dr. Edward Condon, noted physicist and former head of the Bureau of Standards, the investigating group will include Dr. Franklin Roach, astrophysicist; Dr. William Scott, social psychologist; Dr. Stuart Cook, psychologist; Dr. Robert Low, Assistant Dean of the Graduate School; Dr. David Saunders, psychologist. (From the make-up of the group it would appear reasonable to expect that the psychological aspects of the UFO cases would get the most intensive treatment.)

The contract with the University of Colorado is the result of a little-known program which began more than a year before this contract was signed. Shortly after the mass sightings of August and September, 1965, the Air Force quietly established a special panel of its permanent Scientific Advisory Board to investigate and evaluate Project Blue Book's resources and methods of investigation, and to suggest changes which might improve the situation. The board was headed by Dr. Bryan O'Brien, member of the National Academy of Sciences, and included Dr. Carl Sagan, former advisor on extraterrestrial life to the Armed Services. (Dr. Sagan is on record as suggesting that advanced races may already have visited Earth and may have bases somewhere in the solar system, possibly on the averted side of the moon.)

It is interesting to note that this panel, which met on February 3, 1966, dated its report "March, 1966," and released its report (recommending the hiring of outside scientists) only after the flap of March sightings had brought pressure for a Congressional hearing.

Thus it was that the special study group at the University of Colorado came into being ". . . to investigate selected sightings of UFOs." The Air Force will, of course, do the selecting.

During its fifteen-month existence the university group will not deal directly with the public, since it is not set up to handle voluminous correspondence.

Given a free hand and more adequate funds, the University of Colorado group could do a real service by investigating and evaluating some of the more significant sightings objectively.

The final yardstick by which their work will have to be judged, however, will be the quality of the sightings they examine and whether they are permitted to tell the public

47

what they find—if they find something that contradicts the long-established policies of the government in this field.

A possible indication of the trend of the scientists' program may be found in the fact that one of their first actions was to invite Major Donald Keyhoe, NICAP Director, and his assistant, Richard Hall, to Denver, to present some material from NICAP files for possible inclusion in the studies.

"*Swamp gas.*"

4

The police car skidded to a stop.

It was in the Parkman Hill section of Skowhegan, Maine, at 11:25 p.m. on the Friday night of February 11, 1966. In the car were Patrolman Robert Barnes and Special Officer Everett La Pointe.

Ahead of them and at low altitude a bright orange-colored object was moving through the air. The officers estimated that it was about a block ahead of them, that it was about twenty feet long and flat on the bottom, and it seemed to be circular in shape. The officers watched the object until it had moved out of their view behind some houses. While this was taking place they had reported to headquarters what they were seeing.

When they were contacted Sunday by the *Bangor Daily News,* officials at Dow Air Force Base flatly denied any knowledge of anything unusual in the air at the time of the police officers' sighting. The newspaper people knew that Dow's surveillance radar, the most modern equipment available, could follow trucks crossing the runways of the air field or planes sixty miles away at altitudes of forty thousand feet.

Evidently the *Bangor Daily News* had anticipated the brush-off it received from Dow Air Force Base, for it had already spoken with an unidentified official of the Federal Aviation Agency in Bangor.

He disclosed that he had been monitoring the phone line known officially as the "1872 line" which links flight service stations in Augusta, Old Town, and Dow Air Force Base. He told the paper: "Dow radar definitely had something!"

The FAA official added that he had heard the FAA Flight Service unit in Augusta querying Dow about the object, and that Air Force radar (Dow) picked up an intermittent blip over the Skowhegan-Augusta area.

"The blip was making tight turns at low altitude and Dow personnel were not able to determine if the object was an airplane or not."

Another FAA official told the *Bangor Daily News* that military personnel felt that the object was not a conventional aircraft "because it was stationary at times." It had been officially written off as "ground clutter . . . possibly weather," he added.

The spokesman for Dow Air Force Base, when confronted with the statements from the FAA officials, told the paper that there had been an inquiry about the Skowhegan sighting but that the Dow radar had been "unable to track anything."

That was a somewhat different story from the one they had given the Skowhegan police at the time of the sighting. The police blotter shows that, when the police called the base at 2:30 a.m. on the morning of the 12th, they were told: "Both the FAA and Dow say that the radar has been tracking an unknown object on their screen about five or six miles from the Skowhegan area."

On March 24th, near the city of Bangor, a motorist reported to police that a large disc-shaped craft had approached his car and that it had touched down or hovered only a foot or so above the ground. During this near approach, he told authorities, he drew a .22-magnum pistol from the glove compartment of his car and got out of the car where he could see the object better.

"I could see that it was about twenty or twenty-five feet in diameter," said the witness. "It had a clear bubble-type canopy on the top. For a few seconds after I got out of the car it just remained where it was—in the brush. As nearly as I could tell, it was on the ground or else very close to the ground. Then it began to hum or to whine and as it rose it banked slightly in my direction. That was when I fired at it the first time—accidentally. But as it continued to come toward me, rattling the tops of the bushes as it went through them, I fired again. It turned away from me and went down the road about fifty feet in front of my car. There it hovered over a big puddle of water—still making that whining noise. That was when I shot at it the third time and I think I must have hit it, for there was a sping! and its lights flashed up real bright and it took off. I took off too, but I went in the other direction."

Subsequent examination of the spot by police officers revealed a scorched area where the UFO reportedly hovered just above the ground.

In fact, March 24th was a busy day for the UFOs.

In addition to this shooting incident in Maine, a glowing red and white lighted object sailed across a highway about two hundred feet in front of an automobile near Holland, Michigan.

On the same day, a retired Air Force Colonel and several employees of the General Electric Company near New Orleans reported watching a formation of lights maneuvering strangely in the sky, finally making an abrupt change of course before they sped away.

During the late afternoon of March 24th, a professional

53

trapper near Cook, Minnesota, reported to authorities that he had watched an unusual craft about sixty to seventy feet long, with a row of brightly lighted apertures or windows along the side, drop slowly to Earth. A party of investigators on the following day found a deep and long depression in the snow that corresponded to the size and shape of the object which had been described by the witness.

March, the disastrous month for the Air Force UFO explainers, was a very eventful month indeed.

On the 22nd, witnesses at Key West reported that the area around the great Boca Chica Naval Base had been visited by glowing orange-red disc-shaped objects which came streaking in from the ocean, hovered briefly, and then sped on out of sight in the night over the Gulf. And on the following night, near Trinidad, Colorado, witnesses reported to authorities that they had observed two shiny oval-shaped craft flying just above the crest of a ridge. The craft were flat on the bottoms, with rounded convex domes, according to the reports. Also on the night of the 23rd of March, dozens of persons at Joppa, Illinois, said they had watched an elongated object which resembled a cluster of lights with a much brighter light in the middle as the thing maneuvered slowly and silently around over the city.

On March 25th, Toledo (Ohio) police reported watching a large, orbicular, glowing object which hovered for a few moments at treetop level. A farmer and his wife who live near Upper Sandusky, Ohio, told authorities that on the night of the 25th they had seen a glowing spherical or top-shaped thing hovering near the tops of some trees near their home.

Truck drivers near Niles, Michigan, on the night of March 28th had an interesting experience. They told police that a brightly lighted craft, apparently oblong and about thirty to forty feet long, came down and flew parallel to the highway for several minutes. The truck drivers added that, when they blinked the lights of their vehicles, the lights of the UFO blinked in the same sequence, as though to indicate that they understood and accepted the signals.

On the night of March 28th, Federal Aviation Agency control tower operators and other witnesses at Columbus and Atlanta, Georgia, reported watching some oddly maneuvering lights, evidently under intelligent control, carried by oblong craft.

March 30th, Pecos, Texas—an oblong craft, estimated eighty to ninety feet long and twenty-five feet high, reportedly landed near a highway, took off five minutes later. Same night: Long Island, New York—numerous reports of oblong-shaped craft hovering, maneuvering, finally flying out to sea—accompanied by noticeable electromagnetic effects which interfered with automobile ignitions, lights, and broadcast reception.

On the night of April 3rd, a saucer fifty to seventy feet long was seen hovering above a radio transmitter by the station owner and his wife, near Franklin, New Jersey. Same night—Los Angeles—an oblong object with several pairs of lights was seen near International Airport by a veteran helicopter pilot and others.

Iowa City, Iowa—State Police, plus county and city officers, observed a glowing red spherical object, apparently descending, about 11:15 p.m. Cedar Rapids Airport radar picked up a UFO going through the same maneuvers at the same time. And on the night of April 10th, County Sheriffs and local police at Golden, Colorado, reported watching a glowing orange-red object over the mountains east of the city. Hundreds of citizens also saw the thing. Sheriff Dave Courtney told newsmen: "It was definitely something unusual and it wasn't a plane or helicopter."

UFO reports were flooding in from many points around the nation, both before and immediately after the memorable sightings around Dexter and Hillsdale. One experience that would be long remembered befell some police officers in Ohio. Deputy Sheriff Dale Spaur was driving Car 13. Beside him was Special Deputy Barney Neff. They were riding along U.S. 224 between Randolph and Atwater when they spotted an abandoned car parked alongside the road.

A routine check revealed that the car was filled with walkie-talkies and other kinds of radios. Spaur made notes on the matter and walked around to the back of the car to get the license number.

Suddenly he became aware of a heavy humming sound which was rapidly getting louder. Both men turned and saw a disc-shaped craft rising from the woods. The underside gleamed with a brilliant purplish light.

In a matter of seconds the strange craft was over the police car, bathing the two officers in the glow of its blinding lights, which projected a pleasant sensation of warmth, even though the craft was about one hundred fifty feet above them. The two officers noted that the thing was disc shaped, with a low rounded dome on the upper side. They estimated later that it was about fifty feet wide and perhaps fifteen feet thick at the center. It had an antenna or a vertical tube sticking up from the dome at the rear edge. It began moving slowly away from them.

When Deputy Spaur radioed what they were watching,

the dispatcher urged him to shoot it. A moment later the night sergeant came on the radio and instructed Spaur to chase the thing . . . whatever it was. It was already moving away at about twenty miles an hour when Spaur took up the pursuit.

The chase began at Atwater, Ohio, and lasted for eighty-five miles, ending at Freedom, Pennsylvania, when Spaur's car ran out of gas. The speed of the pursuit varied from eighty to one hundred miles per hour. At East Palestine, Ohio, other police heard the chase and Deputy Wayne Huston joined in.

The three police agreed that the object was at about one thousand feet altitude and that it changed course from time to time. It also appeared to wait for the officers to catch up when it began to get too far ahead of them, hovering over the leading car once while waiting for the other to close the distance, apparently. Huston said that the thing appeared to be about the size of an airliner and that the lights from it were blinding when it turned them directly toward the viewers. All told, the chase lasted about fifty-five minutes and involved personnel from seven police departments in various parts of Ohio and Pennsylvania, before the object was lost in the fog at a low angle over the mountains.

Associated Press reported that Air Force reserve pilots stationed at Youngstown, Ohio, were scrambled to chase the object but were unable to do so because of the low speed of the UFO relative to the speeds of the jets. Some of the police reportedly heard the jet pilots talking among themselves during the chase.

Police Chief Gerald Buchert of Mantua, Ohio, heard the chase approaching and went out with his camera. He saw the object (or a similar object) and snapped a picture of it. At first the Air Force asked the Chief not to release the picture, but he says they later told him it was okay to do so.

By way of explanation the Air Force offered the statement that the Deputies had been following a satellite and when it got down close to the horizon they had picked up the planet Venus.

It was probably the first time anyone has been able to keep any manmade satellite in view for fifty minutes, and the first time the National Guard jets at Youngstown have had an opportunity to fly around above the planet Venus.

And what of the picture taken by the Chief of Police?

Just a defect in the film, said the Air Force.

(Deputy Spaur subsequently was the subject of a syndicated newspaper story relating his personal problems which followed this incident, and in some ways stemmed from it. *Spaur's personal troubles however in no way revised or affected the evidence of the incident involving the UFO.*—F.E.)

It becomes evident from examining the sighting reports that there was a flap of major proportions in early 1966 over the United States—but not restricted to this country.

Astronomer Munoz Ferrada reported watching an object over Valparaiso, Chile, on the night of March 24th. The UFO was orange, tinged with blue around the edges, and Munoz told authorities that it flew in circles at an altitude of about five thousand feet for a period of six or seven minutes. He said: "This was definitely under intelligent control—and it was certainly no satellite!"

On the night of May 5th, over Girardot, Colombia (according to the newspaper *El Tiempo* of Bogota), at approximately 9:40 p.m., numerous persons reported watching a circular object or craft crossing the city, giving off an orange glow, with a bluish glow beneath the thing.

"The first person who saw the strange object was Sr. Telesforo Barragan. Later other people saw it clearly. According to the information received, the object illuminated the sky and crossed at supersonic velocity without making a sound.

"This correspondent called by telephone the airport of Flandes [Girardot] where the man in charge confirmed the presence of the strange object giving off the reddish glow, at the time indicated. According to the experts, it might have been an asteroid or a flying saucer. The sight caused naturally great excitement in the city."

(The asteroid hypothesis rules itself out, leaving the UFO as most likely—but with no time factor given we cannot rule out the possibility that it might have been a meteor.—F.E.)

William Keralas, a real estate salesman, was driving along the highway near Naples, Florida, on the night of May 6th when, he later told police, he became aware that he was being followed by a gigantic thing which glowed blue-green. He estimated that the object was about one hundred feet in diameter.

Admittedly alarmed by the approach of the thing, Keralas speeded up to a hundred and fifteen miles per hour . . . but it easily maintained that pace, following him for nearly ten miles along that moonlit highway until it abruptly passed him and disappeared, climbing rapidly.

It was also in Florida, on April 25th, that the Governor of the state and the newsmen with him on his twin-engined plane witnessed a UFO. Of this incident the *NICAP Investigator* says:

"Governor Haydon Burns, campaigning for re-election,

confirmed the sighting but refused to discuss it. This was apparently his second UFO sighting, since a Miami TV station reported last fall, in a documentary, that Gov. Burns had seen one prior to that time.

"Co-pilot Herb Bates first noticed the UFO (on the night of April 25th) as the Convair took off from Orlando headed for Tallahassee. To him the object or objects appeared as two bright yellow globes side by side. At about 6,000 feet in the vicinity of Ocala everyone on board had been alerted and watched the UFO pace the plane on the starboard side. Some said the two bright lights were crescent shaped, with a dimmer connecting column between them. The reddish or yellow-orange lights fluctuated in brightness but were very distinct.

"After several minutes, the Governor ordered his pilot to turn toward the UFO. The lights quickly began an upward climb and then vanished. At this time the capitol bureau chief for the *Tampa Tribune*, Duane Bradford, said, 'The thought occurred to me that this whole UFO business was somewhat less than funny.'

"In addition to the newsmen on board, witnesses included the Governor's executive assistant, Frank Stockton, and Captain Nathan Sharron of the Florida State Police force.

"Central Bureau Chief Bill Mansfield of the *Miami Herald* said the press contingent first learned about the UFO when Governor Burns walked back into the cabin and said, 'We have a UFO out there and I'm going to order the pilot to turn into it!' Confirming the description of the UFO, Mansfield added, 'Something was out there. Something we all saw clearly. Something that has yet to be explained.' "

The UFO activity of the first half of 1966 was by no means restricted to the United States and contiguous areas; the things were being reported on and above Earth from many places.

On Saturday, January 22nd, from the vicinity of Tully, Queensland, New South Wales, came fresh reports of sightings of strange craft . . . and of "saucer nests" where the reported landings in swamps had killed the lush vegetation. Both excessive pressure and heat effects were reportedly evident in the apparent condition of the "nests."

The first "nest" was found on Wednesday, January 19th, by a 27-year-old banana grower, George Pedley, who reported to Australian authorities that he had seen a blue-gray "vaporous looking" craft taking off from the spot on adjoining property that morning. In his statement to the authorities, quoted in the *Sydney Sun Herald* the following day, Pedley described his experience:

"I was driving the tractor through a neighboring property on my way to work. It was about 9 a.m. I heard a loud hissing noise above the engine of the tractor.

"It sounded just like air escaping from a punctured tyre. But the tractor tyres seemed to be okay so I drove on.

"At first I ignored the sound but suddenly I saw a spaceship rise at great speed out of the swamp called Horseshoe Lagoon, about 25 yards in front of me.

"I estimated that it was about 25 feet in diameter and about 9 feet high. It was spinning at a terrific rate as it rose vertically to about 60 feet. Then it made a shallow dive and rose sharply. Travelling at a fantastic speed it headed off in a south-westerly direction. It was out of sight in seconds. I saw no portholes or antennae. There was no sign of life either in or about the ship so far as I could see."

Pedley said that he decided not to say anything about his bizarre experience for fear of ridicule. But on his way home that evening he met a neighbor, Albert Pennisi, who owned the swamp where the UFO had evidently landed. Pedley told him of the strange incident of that morning. Pennisi recalled that on that same morning his dog had "gone mad"—barking and charging repeatedly toward the swamp. But Pennisi had called the animal off and had not tried to ascertain what had caused its excitement.

Encouraged by the reception given to his report by his neighbor, Pedley then drove to a filling station and repeated his account, only to meet with ridicule.

"Then the fun started," he said later. "They were convinced that I was crackers and they told me so!"

Pedley gave his detractors something to think about when he took them to the swamp and showed them the "nest" from which the object had reportedly risen that morning.

It was a circle about thirty feet in diameter in the lush growth of the swamp, evidently the result of great pressure, variously estimated as up to thirty tons. The reeds were crushed and twisted in a clockwise direction. The vegetation which was crushed was dead. That which surrounded it was erect and living. Authorities who visited the spot noted that if the object which caused the "nest" had approached by land the surrounding vegetation would have been crushed and disarranged . . . but the growth was untouched.

On the day following Mr. Pedley's experience, two sightseers, probing around the lagoon, discovered two more apparent "nests."

The men were Tom Warren, a cane farmer of Euramo, and Hank Penning, a school teacher in Tully.

They led authorities to a pair of circular, flattened areas at the edge of the swamp. One of the places was evidently several days old, but the other and smaller (about eight feet in diameter) was much fresher in appearance. Both of these "nests" were about twenty-five yards from the one discovered by Pedley the day before. The smaller spot was crushed into a whorl which was counterclockwise. In the larger circle the reeds were twisted, as in the case of the first "nest," in a clockwise direction.

In these second and third circles, there was evidence of enough weight to crush and kill the vegetation . . . but no indication of heat.

An oddity of the incidents was the discovery, about three feet from the perimeter of the first "nest," of a patch about four feet square from which the grass had been carefully clipped at water level, as though it had been taken for samples. The Royal Australian Air Force asked for samples for testing. When Pennisi and Alf McDonald, Stock Routes Inspector for Northern Queensland waded into the five-foot-deep waters to collect the specimens, they found the chopped-off grass *floating*—with roots attached—as though something had pulled it forcibly from the bottom of the lagoon.

At first McDonald thought that reed-eating grubs might have caused the phenomenon but he also noted that, when grubs are involved, the roots and stems remain as stubble on the lagoon bed.

"There was no stubble here—positively none," said McDonald. "The roots were sucked up whole, and the lagoon floor was smooth."

On January 24th, two more "nests" were found not far from the three which had already been discovered. The fourth and fifth "nests" were found by cane farmer Lou Larchi and his nephew, Van Klaphake of Casula, New South Wales. Larchi told authorities that he felt that the thirty-foot circles he and his nephew had found were considerably older that the ones found the previous week. An interesting aspect of Larchi's discovery was that one of the circles was a mass of floating reeds and grasses, evidently torn from the bottom of the lagoon by terrific suction. The mass was about nine inches thick.

And discovery number six was recorded on February 14, 1966, when two schoolboys, Robert Dennis and Larry Stewart, of Vagoona (near Bankstown) traced out a peculiar pungent odor they had been noticing as they passed a swamp about a mile from the Bankstown Airport, in the western suburbs of Sydney. The boys led authorities to a nearly symmetrical circular area about twenty feet in diameter, identical in description (other than the difference in size) to similar finds in the lagoon near Tully.

In commenting on the promised checking by scientists at Queensland University, who agreed to check the grass samples for possible radioactivity, the *Sydney Telegraph* on January 25th said: "The tests [to be conducted at the University] are similar to those conducted by the U.S. Navy. The USN tests of grass from around the nests [of suspected saucer landings] had a radiation count of 100 per second compared to a normal count of one per second. They also showed that the roots of the grass had been charged."

The testing at the university showed that the grass and reeds from the "nests" had only 1 percent of the radiation of a luminous watch face. Whatever it was that crushed and twisted the vegetation had obviously not been radioactive.

The supposition that it might have been done by a downblast from a helicopter was ruled out by an official of a Brisbane helicopter company, who said:

"It is conceivable that a hovercraft (ground effects) machine might have caused the flattened area, but *not* a helicopter."

Since no hovercraft were known to have been in any of the areas under investigation, that leaves us with only the "nests" . . . to which the UFO proposal alone fits the known facts.

Meanwhile, there was considerable UFO activity all around the globe. Among some of the more interesting cases reported was one from Acarigua, Venezuela, where numerous witnesses reported watching two glowing objects pass over the city on January 19th, at night. One body came from the north, another from the south. When their lines of movement intersected, the city suffered a brief but total electric power blackout.

From Natal, South Africa, in May there came a report of a greenish-blue disc-shaped thing which followed an airliner—and a similar report from Mexico City in April —the 21st—when the pilot of an American Airlines jet checked with the airport regarding a bright object which had followed his plane for several minutes. The tower assured the pilot that there was nothing there.

Different results were obtained on February 8th, when Ken Armstrong, a veteran pilot for Lockheed-Georgia, was returning from a routine mission of instruction. Armstrong was assigned to teach Brazilian Air Force officers in the operations of the new C-30. He was en route to the airport outside Rio de Janeiro with ten Brazilian pilots aboard when he was advised by the tower at the airport that he had been followed by a "white light" for the last thirty miles. Granted permission by the tower, Ken swung the big plane around in order to observe the light—which was then hovering over a church spire about a mile from the airfield. Although the C-30 is by no means a speed plane, Armstrong closed on the object and pursued it for approximately sixty miles. The object had no difficulty keeping well ahead of the plane.

After Armstrong gave up the pursuit and turned back toward the airport, the glowing white object turned and followed *him* again, altering its course and speed from time to time. When the C-30 finally landed, the object halted at about the same place near the church spire as before. Then it seemed to settle slowly for a few minutes and finally veered off and vanished in the distance.

Ken Armstrong is a veteran of many years as an Air Force pilot and as a flier for Lockheed-Georgia. He is thoroughly familiar with aerial oddities, but was admittedly puzzled by this experience. In addition to Armstrong, the glowing white object was observed by the ten Brazilian Air Force pilots who were aboard the C-30 and by the General Motors representative who was also aboard, and by the personnel of the airport tower.

Near Hyderabad, India, in March of 1966, two Army officers reported that their patrol car was forced off the highway and into the ditch by a brightly lighted, humming, circular object which dived repeatedly toward the vehicle.

On the 16th of January, near Kermadien en Balzac, France, M. Eugene Coquil reported to authorities that the presence of a strange, lighted craft which landed on the highway behind his small automobile had caused difficulty with the car's ignition system while the object was close overhead.

One of the strangest and most publicized incidents of the spring flap of 1966 concerned a lady and her husband who were passengers on a British United Airways airliner flying at 9,000 feet, over Cannock in Staffordshire. At the time of the incident the plane was doing about two hundred seventy miles per hour, en route from Manchester to Southampton. The time, 8:10 on the morning of Sunday, March 27th.

Mr. and Mrs. Thomas Oldfield, of No. 5 Gregory Fold, Helmshore, Lancashire, were riding in the rear third of the plane. Suddenly Mrs. Oldfield (Joan, aged 38) noticed what she took to be a jet plane overtaking the plane in which she was riding—except that this "plane" did not seem to have any conventional wings on it. She had an 8mm Minolta movie camera in her lap, loaded with color film, and she twisted around in the seat and ran off several feet of film before the object turned and sped away.

The developed films show quite clearly an oblong shape with what appears to be fins on the top and bottom. The fins seem to be retracting . . . and in the final frames they do not show at all; there is nothing but a dark oval or cigar-shaped object seemingly moving away from the plane.

The films were developed at the Kodak plant in Hemel Hempstead, Herts. Thomas Oldfield told reporters who came to view the pictures that the object seemed to hover for a few seconds below and slightly behind the wing of the plane, then it began retracting its fins, two at the top and two on the bottom. Having done this, he said, it banked sharply and turned away and was quickly out of sight.

Said the Oldfields:

"We have always laughed at these stories of flying saucers but we are not laughing any more. This has convinced us that there is something out there!"

The pictures were copied and printed on the front page of the mass circulation newspaper *News of the World* on Sunday, April 10th, and caused something of a sensation.

This brought the British Air Ministry into the act, and thereby hangs a peculiar tale.

A few days after the Air Ministry became interested they issued an "explanation." The Air Ministry said that another photographer had gone up in the same plane over the same route and had filmed the same object—nothing more, said the Air Ministry, than a reflection of the tail surfaces of the aircraft on the curved window surfaces of the same plane. This film was run on the CBS "UFO" program on May 10th, with the explanation that this solved the case.

Actually, it never came close to solving the case.

What the object was that Mrs. Oldfield filmed, I do not pretend to know—but it was certainly not "a reflection of the tail surfaces of the plane in which she was riding, distorted by the curvature of the surface of the window."

In the first place, had it been nothing more than a reflection of one part of the plane, it could have been photographed right on the ground, for the relationship between the two parts of the plane to the light would be constant; altitude and speed would not enter into the matter.

In the second place, it would be photographically impossible to film a reflection on the *outside* of the window from the *inside* of the plane. In fact, it would not even be possible to see such a reflection from inside the plane, since the reflection would be on the outer surface of the transparent window.

The *only* way the reflection on the *outer* surface of the window could be photographed would be for the picture to be taken from *outside the plane.*

Mrs. Oldfield denies that she was on the wing of the plane at any time during the flight.

"I think it wants to shake hands."

5

In Washington, D.C., the summer of 1950 was no worse than the average summer in that city. But it was just as steamy and sticky and stifling as the summers before and since. And it was on just such an afternoon in that summer that I found myself sweltering in a briefing room at the Pentagon and wondering why I was there, when I could have been in the air-conditioned AFL building, then at 9th and K, Northwest, in which my office was located.

Actually I got into the steamy "briefing room" as the result of a phone call the night before from a friend of mine who held a high rank in the Army. There was to be a special briefing on our plans for space travel and he could get me in if I was interested.

Of course I was interested and I had a free afternoon so I let him book me for the session. It could hardly have been a major problem, for there were only six or seven others in the audience besides me, and two of them left before it was over.

Not until the briefing was completed and I was on my way back to my office did it dawn on me that the program to which I had just listened seemed rather far fetched. In 1950 we were still reassembling those old German V-2 rockets and firing them up a hundred miles or so above White Sands, New Mexico, if all went well. We had no hardware which justified any such complex and long-range dreams as I had just listened to—we were years away from space travel—perhaps decades away from it. That being the case, admittedly, then was it not a bit presumptuous for us to be devoting time and talent to ". . . our seven-point program for conducting a program of space travel involving another planet or planets."

That briefing was conducted by three officers, two of them from the Navy and the other from the Army. In 1950 there was no real censorship on such discussions—nor on the subject. The regulations which were to impose the policy of censorship and deception were almost two years in the future.

Among other aspects of the briefing was the delineation of a carefully thought-out program for conducting ourselves if we found ourselves able to visit another planet inhabited by sentient beings.

Phase One would be the approach. This would take place before we knew whether the planet was inhabited. It would consist of a cautious and careful surveillance from a distance considered safe. If the planet had any satellites which we could use, we would carefully investigate them as possible sites for close-in bases from which to study the planet for the likelihood of intelligent life.

Phase Two would conceivably consist of close-range surveillance of the planet by instrumented probes. These probes would take photographs, gather samples of the atmosphere, and locate the nature and extent of the centers of civilization, if any.

Phase Three: If the results obtained by the instrumented probes seemed to warrant further investigation, that type of craft would be phased out and replaced by faster and more maneuverable manned craft. The purpose

of this change would be to check the performance characteristics of vehicles belonging to the planetary inhabitants
—to test their speed, types of propulsion, and maneuver-
ability as compared to our own.

Phase Four: The really risky phase of the trip is this
phase—where manned craft make near approaches to determine whether the alien beings are hostile and, if so, to
what extent and by what means. Also to check radar locations and locations of military centers, if any.

Phase Five: Brief touchdowns in isolated areas to secure
specimens of plants, animals, and (if possible) specimens
of the intelligent beings themselves.

Phase Six: If we have been successful in acquiring the
information we needed by the preceding steps, we must
now decide on the basis of that knowledge whether to
abandon the project as too risky or otherwise undesirable
—or whether to put into effect the sixth phase of the program. If we decide that the evidence seems to warrant
some kind of eventual contact, direct or indirect, then
phase six would consist of landings and low-level approaches where our craft and their operators could be seen
—but not reached. These approaches would be made
where they could be witnessed by the greatest possible
number of inhabitants. If carried out successfully, this
phase would demonstrate our existence and our nonhostile
nature.

Phase Seven: Referred to by our briefing officers as the
"Overt Contact" phase. This would be the deliberate, carefully planned and executed final step in the program. Contact would not be attempted unless we had excellent reason to believe that it would not be disastrous to either of
the races involved. There are some good reasons why it
might *never* come to pass—even though results of the first

73

six phases might have indicated that it could be physically possible.

Eventually, word of that briefing trickled out via the grapevine. There are somewhat different versions of its content, some of them in publication. Basically, they are very similar to the seven phases which I have set down here. Mine are made from the notes that I took that day. I do not pretend that they are infallible, for I may have erred from time to time in trying to keep up with the tempo of the discussion. There may even have been other programs—and other briefings at other times. I can only say to you that this is the substance of the one which I had the good fortune to attend that steamy afternoon in 1950. And to my knowledge it bears a working resemblance to the other versions which are extant . . . and to some evidence which we will examine.

Since we had no space program in those days, and very little prospect of one, I wondered why the briefing had been held and why the seemingly premature emphasis on that topic.

At no time during the two-and-one-half-hour briefing was there any reference whatever to what were then called "flying saucers." And it was some weeks after the briefing before I began to wonder if that was what they had been talking about, trying to alert us what to expect if the strange objects finally proved to be spacecraft, as so many persons (including many in government) already suspected.

The more I pondered and the closer I looked and the deeper I dug—the more firm became my conviction that the officers at that briefing *really had been* trying to alert us to the probable development of the UFO problem. If so, they had done a surprising job of forecasting—or projecting.

Let's look at the record.

Phase One, you will recall, was the approach—the slow, cautious, long-range surveillance to determine whether the planet under observation was inhabited by sentient beings.

The record: For thousands of years man has recorded cases of strange craft in the skies. From some of these craft living beings have ventured forth, according to the accounts in the Bible and ancient scrolls. These visits were of brief duration for the most part; they were very widely spaced in time. If they were indeed visitations by intelligent beings from elsewhere in the universe, the visitors probably found little to interest them on our planet: they would conceivably have marked it down as "inhabited, but primitive" and noted it for future reference.

In that case they would have noted that Earth had a satellite, large enough and near enough to be used as a base for short-range operations, when and if such operations were warranted by our developments. On Earth they found the beings, developing as the ages passed by, needing only time to make use of what they had.

In my preceding book on this subject, *Flying Saucers— Serious Business*, I have recounted briefly the strange sequence involving the satellites of Mars and the rash of phenomena on our moon which followed their appearance. Let it suffice here to point out that in 1877 two bright satellites were found to be orbiting Mars. Not only were they brighter than the planet itself (as though they were of other material) but they were seen where no other satel-

75

lites had been detected in more than a hundred years of watching.

There are other peculiarities about the Martian moons, some of which lead some scientists to the suspicion that the satellites are of artificial origin. That is mere scientific deduction and hypothesis; we are more concerned with the facts—with the thousands of examples of geometric patterns of lights on the dark portion of the moon between 1879 and 1882. They had never been seen there before . . . nor have they been reported since. But the astronomers who reported them to the British Astronomical Society did so in the hope that these bizarre patterns of lights were attempts by somebody to signal us. In other words, they thought somebody was using our moon as a base—an idea which also concerned our Armed Services as recently as December, 1962.

Phase Two: Close-range surveillance of the planet by instrumented probes.

The record: After a dearth of reports of unconventional aerial craft covering a thirty-year period, pilots in military aircraft during World War II began reporting strange disc-shaped objects, generally not exceeding three or four feet in diameter, which played about the fighter planes. These things we suspected to be some sort of enemy device; the enemy thought they were ours. For want of a better name, we called them "foo fighters." They were harmless. They were highly maneuverable. They were impervious to machine-gun fire on the extremely rare occasions when they could be hit at all. As one fighter pilot said to me: "They seemed to be well-trained pieces of mechanized curiosity!"

As early as 1943, the British had set up a small organization to gather information on these objects. It was under the direction of Lieutenant General Massey, and it had been inspired to some extent by the reports of a spy who was in reality a double agent, working under the direction of the Mayor of Cologne. He had confirmed that the foo fighters were not German devices but that the Germans thought they were Allied ranging instruments, which of course the British knew they were not. The British Air Ministry, in 1966, told me that the Massey Project was officially terminated in 1944. Perhaps it is only coincidence that the double agent was exposed and executed in the spring of 1944.

But the foo fighters were very much in evidence, even though official British interest is said to have waned. Both British and American fliers reported the objects. Typical was this example from a bombing attack on the great German industrial complex at Schweinfurt on October 14, 1943. The detailed discussion of the phenomenon is taken from a signed report made by Major E. R. T. Holmes, F.L.O., 1st Bombardment Squadron, to the Minister of Information 15, War Office, Whitehall, London, under date of October 24, 1943. (Mission No. 115 in the British records.)

Major Holmes reports that as the bombers of the 384th group (American-made B-17s) took positions for their bombing runs on the target, the German fighter planes were all *below* the bombers. This is an important point and it was brought out by the unanimous replies of the pilots and other crew members of the bombers—*no German fighters were above them at the time of the phenomenon.*

As the B-17s roared on their bombing path, they found themselves closing rapidly with a formation of small, silvery discs. The objects were very numerous—"scores of them"—and they were flying headlong toward the bombers. They were gliding downward under apparent control and on a collision course.

One bomber pilot told Intelligence interviewers later that the objects barely missed his right wing as he went through their formation. Another pilot said that one of the things struck the tail surfaces of his bomber a glancing blow but without apparent effect. Two other aircraft in the same formation also flew through the formation of small shiny discs (estimated at about an *inch thick and four inches in diameter*) without suffering any apparent damage. Twice later, while the bombers were dropping their bombs, they were visited by these mysterious little discs, but none of the fliers had any idea where they came from, or what they were.

The foo fighters became ubiquitous and were a well-known phenomenon by the end of the war. From their actions both over Europe and the Orient, they gave the impression of being interested in the capabilities of our planes but they also remained well aloof from any downright involvement in the activities. The records are replete with mention of them. It was only after the end of World War II that the antagonists discovered that whatever they were—or whatever they wanted—they did not belong to anyone involved in the war itself. The foo fighters seemed to be curious—and they were so small and so highly maneuverable that they were safe from the weaponry carried by the planes.

If, as it seems reasonable to conclude, the tiny discoid objects which flitted about among the planes during World War II were instrumented probes of a highly specialized nature, then the larger discs which made their appearance in numbers in May of 1946 were a logical extension and amplification of the program which seems to have had its genesis in the war.

In May of 1946, northwestern Russia, Sweden, Finland, Norway, and Denmark began to report strange objects flipping around in the skies. It was just one year after man exploded his first atomic device at Alamogordo, which may be coincidental—then again it may not. But the objects which zipped around in the night skies of the northwestern corner of Europe in the spring of 1946 were first called "ghost rockets," although that name did not fit any of their performance characteristics. When they became daytime visitors a few weeks later, it was noted that they were circular in shape and rather like soup plates in contour. And as the governments involved soon discovered—whatever the things were—they could easily outmaneuver any plane that could be put into the air against them. They could—and they did.

The appearance of the same type of object in numbers over the western hemisphere in the late spring of 1947 would seem to conform to Phase Two as outlined in the briefing in 1950—an amplification of the approach by the use of instrumented probes which could gather information without jeopardy to the investigators.

I wish to caution that there is not—at least yet—any proof that the "flying saucers" of 1946-1953 were merely amplifications of the tiny foo fighters of World War II. But neither is there any other hypothesis which might explain their timing, their purpose, and their appearance in conformity with the known facts.

Phase Three: If the evidence accumulated to this point seemed to warrant further investigation on the part of the operators of the UFOs, the briefing informed us that the craft in use in the preceding phases would be replaced by faster and more maneuverable craft, capable of checking the performance characteristics of our vehicles.

After the little foo fighters vanished from the scene the so-called "flying saucers" appeared. This type of UFO was generally about twenty-five feet in diameter, circular, with a low dome and a narrow rim. In a few cases (for instance, around Washington, D.C., in mid-1952) some of the discs were described by pilots in interceptor craft as being only about two feet in diameter. (See statement by Wilbert B. Smith, head of the Canadian UFO Project, on page 83 of *Flying Saucers—Serious Business.*) But around the globe, the most credible reports from the most competent witnesses described a disc about twenty-five feet in diameter. There is not a single credible report of a living creature being seen in or around one of this "flying saucer" type of UFOs. These objects were evidently instrumented craft, representing an advanced technology, which had completed their mission by the summer of 1953.

In September of 1953 the phasing out of the "flying saucer" type of UFO was called to the attention of the Air Technical Intelligence personnel by an article in the *Air Force Intelligence Manual,* published by the Air Force. The article was illustrated by two "artist's conceptions" of the new type of UFO which was then coming into use. It showed a double-convex disc, similar to two rounded bowls stuck together at the rims. And most significantly, it also showed that this new type of UFO had a transparent dome located in the center of the upper dome—unmistakably for the use of the operators.

(The last authentic photograph of a disc-shape UFO to my knowledge was that made over Rouen, France, on March 5, 1954, by a French fighter pilot. It looked almost identical to the object photographed by a farm wife, Mrs. Paul Trent, over McMinnville, Oregon, in May of 1950. By the time the photo was taken over Rouen, the "saucer-type disc" had become passé—evidently phased out and replaced by the double-convex types pictured in the *Air Technical Manual*.)

An excellent early account of operators around a UFO was that sworn to by Otto Linke, former Mayor of Hasselbach, Saxonia, in the spring of 1952. In a statement to the British and American military authorities in West Germany, Linke described the landed craft as resembling a "big warming pan without a handle," presumably a double-convex type and certainly not a disc- or saucer-shaped object. Linke described the creatures (two) as looking like tiny men, dressed in shiny garments and wearing transparent helmets. Upon becoming aware of the presence of Linke and his daughter, the creatures hastened into the craft through the top, and a few seconds later it took off with a hissing or whistling sound, not so loud as a falling bomb, as Linke and his daughter described it.

The appearance of "manned" double-convex UFOs in 1953 coincided with a rash of reports of close-range encounters involving the UFOs and various types of manmade craft. If they were checking out our equipment, they were doing it very systematically and very thoroughly.

The year 1954 came in with a rush of UFOs. In Brazil they seemed especially active, buzzing automobiles along lonely stretches of highway, making near approaches to planes, interfering with electric power transmission. They gave every indication of being obsessed by curiosity about man and his works.

It was in 1954 that many landings were reported, including the now famous Quaroubles, France, case involving a young steelworker named Marius DeWilde, who saw some small manlike creatures in shiny suits and helmets who took off in a craft that was resting on the railroad tracks. Authorities who investigated found deep indentations in the rail cross timbers where DeWilde said the craft had been. Engineers estimated that the marks had been made by an object that weighed at least thirty tons.

From Thailand, in May of 1954, Captain Uthai Lunayatjata reports that one night while he was instructing a flight of three planes piloted by trainees, he went up in a plane around midnight with one of the trainees ". . . and climbed to about three thousand feet. Then we leveled off and set a course to the west. We made a 180-degree turn and flew directly toward the town of Korat. It was a clear night with no clouds and no moon.

"When we had almost reached the town I saw something strange in the sky. It appeared to be an orange ball about six feet in diameter. I first saw it about 1,500 feet ahead and approaching our plane on a parallel course to our right. And at the same time the fiery ball seemed to move at very great speed and as it passed our plane I calculated its speed at 800 to 1,000 miles per hour. Thinking that it might have been another plane of some kind I phoned the control tower and was told that no other planes were in the area.

"In order to keep the orange fireball in sight we began making a 180-degree right hand turn and it was then that I became aware of a smaller fireball, blue in color, which appeared to be attached to the right side of the orange object. Both appeared to move as one. Before we had completed our turn the fireball had made a fast half-circle and was only about 600 feet behind our tail. It slowed down and accompanied us for some distance. Our normal speed was about 140-160 miles per hour. It seemed strange that this glowing thing could travel at such tremendous speed and then reduce to such slow speed.

"At this close range we were able to see that the center of the orange fireball was really quite dark, as though nothing was there. But the blue colored light seemed to be a ring around some object but the glare of the blue was too bright for us to discern the shape or substance of the thing. After twenty seconds it increased its speed and flew ahead of us, making a climbing right hand turn. I put on full throttle and followed but had to abandon the chase at 5,000 feet because I could not get near it. The object continued to climb rapidly at very high speed until it became invisible in the sky."

In 1954, reports poured in from all parts of the world of strange objects which could outfly jets with tantalizing ease. From all the oceans, ships' officers reported near-approaches of strange objects which sometimes seemed to cause interference with the electronic gear and the electromagnetic compasses in particular. Motorists who reported near-approaches of UFOs generally reported that they had difficulties with their ignition systems and lights. (In Brazil, a small automobile was overtaken by a UFO which swept overhead so close to the car that the car rose into the air and flipped into the ditch, fortunately with little injury to either the car or the occupants. Passing motorists witnessed and confirmed the incident to authorities.)

Although the advent of the new-type UFOs in late 1953 had led to increased activity around the world in 1954, the United States seemed to be of especial interest to the operators of the strange craft.

The Air Force struggled manfully to carry out the pol-

83

icy of deception and censorship which had been imposed upon it in 1952. It dutifully issued one of its "statistical reports," which asserted that in the first four months of 1954, it had received only eighty-seven UFO reports. On that same day the Air Technical Intelligence Center at Wright-Patterson Field in Dayton issued a statement which said that 1954 was the biggest year on record for UFOs—that they were receiving reports of sightings at the rate of more than seven hundred cases per week!

One of the most interesting cases—and one of the best documented—was that of May 13, 1954.

My information on this first case comes from the electronics specialists who were involved. I was based in Washington at the time, and several of the parties who reported to me were personal friends of mine.

On that day, shortly before noon, a team of experts were putting the finishing touches on a new type of radar. They noticed that it was recording some type of object at great altitude—something of unusual size. They double-checked by switching on another unit, and it too began tracking the same object. They were able to determine that it was at least two hundred fifty feet in diameter, about fifteen miles above Washington, and that it was moving from point to point around a rectangular pattern in the sky at about two hundred miles per hour. After three hours of this maneuvering, under the scrutiny of several government radar installations, the object finally moved toward the west and disappeared from the screens.

That was Case Number One for May 13, 1954.

About 12:45 that same afternoon, two police officers assigned to the National Airport just across the Potomac from Washington, spotted two large glowing oval objects which approached the airport and maneuvered over both the airport and part of the city of Washington. Their presence was confirmed by Military Air Transport. Newsmen who questioned an Air Force spokesman in the Pentagon were told to call the things Unidentified Flying Objects. The things had been seen intermittently between 12:45 and 2:00 p.m.

Two cases on the same day over the national capital.

I carried both reports on my nationwide news commentary over the Mutual Network that night.

The second report appeared in just one edition of the *Washington Post*.

The lid was on.

It was against this background of UFO activity of unprecedented intensity over the nation—and especially over Washington, D.C.—that General Nathan Twining, Chief of Staff of the Air Force, spoke to an audience in Amarillo, Texas, on May 15, 1954—only forty-eight hours after the two cases I have just mentioned.

General Twining made a surprising digression from the subject of his speech to say: "The best brains in the Air Force are working on this problem of Unidentified Flying Objects, trying to solve this riddle."

A remarkable utterance from a man who knew whereof he spoke. A very timely remark, too, in the circumstances.

Yes, 1954 was an important year in the annals of UFO activity. In February of that year, the meeting at the Roosevelt Hotel in Hollywood between Military Air Transport Intelligence officials and the Airline Pilots Association had reached an agreement to stop airline pilots from making public reports on UFO sightings.

On May 13th, the two radar and visual sightings over Washington, D.C., which I have just detailed.

85

On May 15th, General Nathan Twining's remarkable remark at Amarillo.

On May 17th, four veteran National Guard pilots in jets over Dallas, Texas, engaged in a game of high-altitude tag with sixteen UFOs before the jets were outmaneuvered and outdistanced. Reported in *Dallas Herald* on May 25th. Not reported by any news service.

On May 31st, Fifth Air Force officials in Japan confirmed reports that U.S. jet fighter planes in Korea had been pursuing and shooting at UFOs.

On June 9th, Colonel Frank Milani, Director of Civil Defense in Baltimore, issued public demand that Air Force lessen its secrecy regarding UFOs.

June 10th. Air Force denies Colonel Milani's implications of secrecy and censorship; claimed only eighty-seven UFO reports received in first four months of that year. ATIC at Dayton refuted Air Force claim when Deputy Commander of Intelligence Colonel John O'Mara admitted that more than a thousand scientists were working on the problem and added that more than seven hundred UFO cases were being received each week ". . . heaviest rate of sightings on record."

July 9, 1954. Front-page headline in the *Wilmington* (Delaware) *Morning News:* 100 MYSTERY OBJECTS SPOTTED HERE—"Air Force permits Ground Observer Corps to release data on phenomena sighted here and confirmed elsewhere." The article disclosed that the ground observers had been watching these objects and reporting them to the Baltimore Filter Center where the Air Force studied the reports (and where Colonel Milani got the material for his blast!). On July 5th, just four days before the *Wilmington Morning News* broke the story, the Air Force had officially identified one of the things as "an Unidentified Flying Object."

From South America in 1954 came a flood of sighting reports, to be added to the hundreds which poured in from Europe, North Africa, the Near East, and Japan. Germany, Italy, Sweden, and Yugoslavia in 1954 joined the list of nations which were admittedly engaged in serious probes of these objects.

A study of these reports indicates that the UFOs were conducting a systematic and cautious study of man's modes of travel. They also visited every radar base, communications center, and industrial complex of importance—and demonstrated an increasing interest in electric generating installations.

All in all, a summary of UFO cases from credible sources in 1954, after the advent of the double-convex type of craft, leads to the conclusion that they were indeed engaged in the estimates of what the briefing had specified as Phase Four—but with overtones of Phase Five.

By 1955, it had been well established that we were dealing with specialized craft of unknown origin and purpose. There had been no indication of any hostility on their part nor had there been any indication of any apparent desire to establish communications with man. We were aware of their presence, of their general appearance, of their program of intensive surveillance. But where they came from—and why—and how they propelled themselves were matters which eluded us then—and to a large extent —still do.

Dr. Hermann Oberth, father of the German rocket program, investigated these UFOs for that country, and at a news conference he declared:

"There is no doubt in my mind that these objects are interplanetary craft of some sort. I and my colleagues are confident that they do not originate in our solar system but we feel that they may use Mars or some other body as a sort of way-station."

During the summer of 1954, hundreds of professional astronomers flocked to the southern hemisphere to view Mars under optimum conditions. From that portion of Earth the telescopes can be pointed toward Mars without having to scan it through the distorting layers of atmosphere which bother the viewing from the northern hemisphere. It is for this reason that most of the astronomers who have reported seeing the lines on Mars have done so while viewing the planet from our southern hemisphere. During this study of Mars in 1954, Dr. E. C. Slipher of Lowell Observatory used the fine big telescope at Bloemfontein, South Africa, and at the conclusion of his work he declared that there could no longer be any doubt that life of some kind existed on Mars. Slipher and other astronomers took thousands of pictures during the study. But the official statement from the Mars committee was delayed for months because the scientists could not agree on what they had seen—or what it meant.

The upshot of it was that a program which had been instituted with the possible goal of settling the controversy ended in an equivocal statement which settled nothing; it merely postponed "the next big episode," as they used to say in the movie serials. We were led to believe that once we could get some close-up pictures of Mars—ah! Then we would be able to tell——.

If you will bear with me for doing so, I should like to digress here from our study of the UFO procedures and the seven-phase program discussed at the briefing—to develop the Martian study and its peculiar twists and turns.

We have just seen how the 1954 Mars Program ended in disagreements among the scientists involved.

As a fascinating and perhaps important portion of our multibillion-dollar space program, we launched a device designed to photograph Mars and to transmit the pictures back to Earth. Officially designated as Mariner 4, it took off from Cape Kennedy in November, 1964, on a curving flight which put it alongside Mars in July, 1965. Its phenomenally accurate path was a marvelous scientific achievement. The pictures it sent back by television were equally remarkable, another scientific milestone.

But Mariner 4's performance—and the subsequent performance of some of the scientists involved—left fresh mysteries to be resolved.

As the probe neared Mars, the public was told that it might be months before any of the pictures would be released! The uproar which followed that inept statement brought a prompt follow-up which stated that "selected" pictures would be released shortly after they were received.

Then came the official declaration that the cameras on Mariner 4 would be turned off after Picture No. 7 to avert possible erasure. Instead, the cameras continued to take and transmit, without interruption, at least twenty-two pictures.

Unmentioned in the public statements, and unexplained to this day, is the fact that something very strange happened to Mariner 4 as it passed behind the planet Mars.

The speed of the probe was carefully controlled; it had to be very precise to be at the right place at the right time —and it was. Mariner 4 was moving at eleven thousand miles per hour when it entered the shadow of Mars. The tracking station at Tidbinbilla, Australia, had been alerted to expect Mariner 4 to come out of the Martian shadow in a very precise fifty-two minutes and thirty-two seconds after it entered. But something happened while the device was behind Mars. It did not reappear until sixty-four minutes and thirty-six seconds had dragged past. It had slowed down so much and so quickly that it had actually lost slightly more than twelve minutes while it was hidden from us by Mars!

There has been no scientific explanation of this facet of the Mariner 4 performance.

Also please note that when Mariner 4 reappeared from behind Mars and began transmitting the puny little signals which would eventually be electronically rebuilt into photographs, the anxious experts at Tidbinbilla, about twenty-five miles from Canberra, found themselves confronted with still another riddle. They were picking up bothersome signals—officially called "anomalies" in their records—and there was a UFO hovering only a few miles away, between the tracking station and the Canberra Airport.

As long as the glowing, oval-shaped UFO hovered there, the Tidbinbilla equipment was plagued with the anomalous signals. When a Royal Australian Air Force jet was scrambled (the pilot said the UFO just "flipped up and went away and left me. I was not in its class, that is certain!") the UFO vanished at great altitude and the anomalous signals ceased to interfere with the reception.

In addition to the pilot of the jet interceptor just mentioned, the six members of the Control Tower at the airport also watched the UFO, along with many civilians, two pilots of airliners, and various military fliers. And of course the personnel of the tracking station itself, some of whom reportedly observed the UFO through binoculars. The incident received wide coverage in the Australian and European press but got little more than a mention in the United States.

Picture No. 1 transmitted by Mariner 4 was distinguished by a large white marking which was promptly dubbed "the crow's foot." It was reminiscent of the immense "W" which had been repeatedly photographed in the Martian atmosphere by Dr. Slipher, ten years before. Whatever it was, the Mariner 4 Picture No. 1 was "reprocessed"and reissued minus its most distinguishing feature.

The pictures which were released for public view showed a rugged, crater-scarred planet. This came as a surprise to those of us who had been led to believe that Mars was a vast, barren desert, given over to great sand and dust storms of such magnitude that they even colored the thin atmosphere, etc. The Mariner pictures which were made public gave no hint of the softening effect of either sand or dust. They looked, in fact, as one critic observed, more like enlargements of a small area of the moon, made from a negative which reversed the details from left to right.

I believe that most people awaited the Martian pictures in the hope that they might reveal something definitive relative to the existence—or nonexistence—of the lines which Giovanni Virginio Schiaparelli in 1877 called "canali," generally misinterpreted as "canals." Their reported patterns and changing colors would seem to indicate that they were the product of some form of intelligent planning—if they existed.

The first official statements regarding the Mariner 4 pictures asserted bluntly that the pictures showed no trace of the lines and nothing to indicate the presence of life on Mars.

That statement was false.

NICAP revealed the facts in its official publication for January-February, 1966, under the headline MARS "CANALS" REAL, NEW FILM REPORTS SHOW.

The breakthrough evidently began with a statement by famed astronomer Dr. Clyde Tombaugh, who reported to the American Association for the Advancement of Science that in seven of the twenty-two pictures taken by Mariner 4, he had found "canal" streaks and "oasis" spots. The "oases" to which Dr. Tombaugh refers are the juncture points of the "canals," where several of them intersect, evidently by design and not in conformity to any natural effect. All of these markings, the astronomer declared, coincided with similar markings he had personally seen in telescopic studies of the planet and in maps of Mars made by other astronomers.

NICAP reports that copies of the Mariner photos showing the straight-line "canals" were shown to that organization by Dr. Frank Salisbury of Colorado State University, a noted exobiologist who has analyzed the evidence for traces of life on Mars. NICAP reports that the lines appeared clearly and unmistakably in Mariner Photos No. 11 and No. 12.

Professor Robert B. Leighton, in charge of the Mariner 4 television picture operations, told the American Physical Society on January 27, 1966, in New York City, that the films were still being studied in the hope that they might yield more information regarding the strange "canals." He added that, since it was not known exactly where the cameras were pointing when they took the pictures, it was not possible to pinpoint the lines to specific

Martian areas. And what about the NASA report on the 1965 Mars pictures? Professor Leighton said that it would not include any information regarding the "canals."

Thus it came about that Dr. William Pickering confirmed that Mariner 4 *had* sent back pictures of the lines on Mars, after all. Since he is the head of the Jet Propulsion Laboratory, which controlled the Mariner 4 operation for NASA, this meant an official about-face from the same outfit which had previously denied that such lines had been photographed.

The deplorable part of the Mariner 4 photos is that so much of the information had to be pried out of the officials who possessed it—at public expense. In that respect the Mars photos were commonplace, rather than unique.

The phase of intensive surveillance and checking out of man's vehicles seems to have flourished from the advent of the double-convex UFOs in mid-1953, to have reached a peak in 1954, and then to have tapered off, at least over the highly industrialized nations, in late 1955. By that time shooting at them had also tapered off as official U.S. policy. Our jets still pursued them when the UFOs appeared over important military areas but we no longer used weapons against them, except on rare occasions when weapons could be used with little danger to humans, as in the case of ships at sea. In 1963, one of our missile ships stationed in the South Atlantic launched a surface-to-air missile against a hovering UFO, *but only after having been ordered to do so from base.* My source, one of the missile ship's officers, tells me that the missile scored a hit and the UFO was destroyed. The subsequent search for debris was futile.

Despite the ofttimes hostile attitude of human beings— especially the more "civilized" humans—the operators of the UFOs seem to have decided that activity corresponding to Phase Six (as it was described to us at that briefing in 1950) could be carried out.

This, in our proposed program, would consist of landings or near-landings, where the craft could be seen but not reached; of making our presence and nonhostile nature known to the greatest possible number of inhabitants of the planet under study.

Have the UFOs engaged in such activity?

A careful study of the global record of the UFOs leads me to the conclusion that they have made such appearances, and that the program is working, if our estimate of it is correct. This only becomes apparent when the sighting reports from all over Earth are placed in chronological sequence. The occasional landing reports of the mid-1950's have been continuing. In many cases, even as recently as the spring of 1967, the UFOs have been reported by credible witnesses as operating at very low altitude over relatively small bodies of water (for example, Wanaque Reservoir, N.J.) where the UFO's were clearly visible but where men could not reach them. Those bodies of water simply provide the UFOs with a safe stage for displaying themselves. They have also been seen around ships at sea under excellent viewing conditions. And around passenger planes in mid-air—still another case where they could be seen, but not reached. If that was their goal, they were attaining it despite steadfast official denial of their existence. By the summer of 1966, a Gallup poll across the nation indicated that at least five million Americans were willing to admit that they had seen strange objects which they felt were UFOs.

One of the great landmark dates in the unfolding UFO mystery was the memorable night of August 2-3, 1965.

From the Dakotas to New Mexico and Arizona, tens of

thousands of persons in the Great Plains states stood out on that warm clear night and watched an awe-inspiring aerial exhibition. Sometimes the lights moved in formation. Sometimes it was a single pulsating light. Sometimes they were high; sometimes so low that they could be photographed by amateur camera operators. They were tracked on radar—both civil and military—according to State Police reports. They changed formation from time to time; they changed speed; and they changed color and size.

It was a magnificent aerial display that brought out an estimated quarter of a million viewers. Among that audience were many competent and credible observers, including numerous newsmen in the various media.

Something spectacular was taking place up there—what was it? That was the question that was put to the Air Force next morning.

The official answer?

"Four stars in the constellation Orion."

Professional astronomers promptly stomped that under foot. Among them was Dr. Robert Risser, who debunked the official "answer" by pointing out the fact that at that time the constellation Orion was visible only from the other side of Earth!

That faux pas of August 3, 1965, was the turning point which I had long awaited. I felt that it had fully exposed the real caliber of the official "explanations" of most UFO sightings. And I also felt that the existing policy of censorship had at last been recognized by the news media.

On that day I sat down to begin writing my book about the UFO phenomenon, based on nineteen years of study and research. As the recipient of a great deal of ridicule during all those years I welcomed the change in editorial attitude. Most of all, I was gladdened by the change in

95

public attitude which had preceded the long-awaited breakthrough.

For a title I took the title of a secret memorandum which the Inspector General of the Air Force had sent to all Base Commanders in December of 1959—"UFOs Serious Business." Because most people still spoke of the things and thought of them as the long outmoded saucers, I transposed the title to *Flying Saucers—Serious Business*. It was published in June of 1966 and became the first book on UFOs to make the best seller lists and eventually became the biggest selling book on the subject ever written to date. This tremendous public acceptance also included my RCA Victor album of the same title as the book. Their success is due to the fact that the public was eager to know what was known about the subject—that the public did not accept the official statements as valid answers.

The most immediate effect of the discredited explanation to which I have just referred was a rash of irate editorials demanding to know the reasons for the obvious secrecy and the official deception relative to UFOs.

The closing months of 1965 were replete with UFO reports which were of a nature conducive to widespread exposure of the objects. If they were indeed trying to make their presence known to the greatest number of persons, they were pursuing a program that was accomplishing that assignment.

The year 1966 opened with innumerable sightings, including the one at Wanaque Reservoir in New Jersey, where two Mayors, numerous guards and police, and hundreds of civilians watched the object maneuvering at low altitude over the frozen reservoir. The reservoir guards reported that where the thing hovered and sent down shafts of light onto the ice, they found holes up to nine feet in diameter melted through the ice. The first official explanation that this was a special helicopter was subsequently withdrawn and replaced with a suggestion that it might have been Venus or Jupiter. If so, this must have been one of their closest approaches to Earth, since the witnesses agreed that the object came within twenty feet of the reservoir.

The same reservoir was revisited by a similar UFO (Pardon me—planet!) in October of 1966 but, as I have reported elsewhere, the rerun had a different ending.

Then in March of '66 the Air Force blew itself out of the explanation business when the Michigan swamp gas exploded in their faces. That it was the brain child of Project Blue Book seems likely enough, but the upshot of it was that it tarred the Air Force in the public prints, and led to Congressional demands for an investigation.

Whether by chance or by plan, the UFOs were showing themselves to a great many good witnesses and at close range.

In the Wanaque case alone, the witnesses included newspaper editor Howard Ball, of the *Paterson News*; Police Officer Jack Wardlaw, Police Sergeant David Cisco, Patrolman Charles Theodora, and Sergeant George Dykman.

On January 3, 1966, an exceptionally competent observer was added to the long list of credible witnesses. He was Lieutenant Colonel Robert B. Staver, now retired and living in Los Altos, California. During his many years in the Army, he was one of three Army specialists assigned to rocket work during World War II. He was in charge of the rocket projects at Aberdeen and was the expert sent to Germany to investigate Nazi rocket operations and procedures.

Lieutenant Colonel Staver reported to NICAP that he

had observed a group of brilliantly lighted objects moving over Los Altos at an estimated one thousand to twelve hundred miles per hour. The irrefutable control under which the things moved ruled out the possibility that they were meteors, and he added that shortly after the objects had vanished over the ocean he noticed searchlights sweeping the sky, as though trying to pick them up, but Lieutenant Colonel Staver noted that the searchlight beams were very pale in comparison to the exceptional brilliance of the UFOs which had just passed over.

By the summer of 1966 multitudes of persons had seen some very strange objects in the air and, in many cases, on the ground. Despite official denials, it was becoming increasingly apparent to many persons that there was something unusual up there; something that had a source and a purpose and a propulsion system that was literally out of this world.

Let us once again examine the evidence.

"I don't understand it. They loved us in Michigan."

6

By way of emphasizing the international scope of the UFO problem, this headline from the *Australian Dominion,* June 7, 1966:

CONSTABLES . IN . CHASE . WITH . FLYING . SAUCER

On the previous evening, says the paper, hundreds of persons in the community of Grafton (near Sydney) watched a UFO maneuvering at low altitude while two police officers followed it around the community in their patrol car.

Constables E. Mercer and P. Woodman were sitting in the Grafton Police Station at 8 p.m. when they received a call from a man who reported what he called "a funny looking thing" in the sky and suggested that the officers might want to take a look.

They did. With considerable misgivings the officers went outside and they too saw the bright object hovering where the caller had reported it. The officers trained binoculars on it and they could detect a large ring of light which changed slowly from white to red and back to white. It appeared to be at fifteen hundred feet altitude and it was being watched from all sides by excited residents who were phoning to report. The police board was jammed with calls from witnesses.

The two officers used a police car to follow the thing across the city. It stopped from time to time and made very leisurely progress until it was slightly southwest of Grafton. Then it suddenly accelerated and darted away at high speed.

The officers and other residents had the thing in view for about two hours.

The Rome (Italy) *Daily American* of June 17th describes a celestial phenomenon which had occurred there the preceding night. The paper reports that thousands of citizens of Rome witnessed a series of unidentifiable lights in the sky to the south of the city.

The first object was moon-shaped, radiating all the colors of the rainbow as it sailed serenely across the night sky. In all, three such lights were seen within a few seconds of each other, following the same paths and each succeeding light dropping lower toward the horizon, diminishing in size and intensity as they did so.

As described, these objects could not have been either meteors or manmade satellites.

Two scientists at Abingdon, Berkshire, reported watching a strange object in the sky on June 17th. *The Observer* identifies the witnesses as Dr. R. S. Gilmore and P. D. Wroath, who first saw it about ten minutes before 8 p.m. They had it under continuous observation for one and a half hours, part of that time through a six-inch reflector telescope.

They described it as a shining cone of light . . . an elliptical thing with a central domelike structure. It also seemed to have three equally spaced headlights. It was reflecting sunlight and, said the scientists, ". . . showed shadow and contrast as a solid body would."

Eyepieces with a magnification of up to two hundred

diameters were used during the course of the observation.

Since the object was receiving sunlight forty minutes after sunset, it was possible to calculate that it was at least twenty-eight miles from the viewers. Its altitude was calculated to have been at least seven and a half miles, and the size of the image in the telescope indicated that the thing was more than sixty feet wide.

Five other persons were invited to view the object because of what the paper called "its extraordinary appearance."

The object changed speed from time to time, hovered for thirty minutes, and was finally lost in the gathering gloom in a bank of low-hanging clouds.

The scientists involved in this sighting are identified as an amateur astronomer and a member of the British Astronomical Association, P. D. Wroath, and a physicist at the Science Research Council at Harwell, Dr. R. S. Gilmore.

The shape, motion, and configuration of this object rule out the conventional explanations that it was a balloon, a satellite, a meteor, or a flock of birds.

And it was a bit too high for swamp gas.

You will probably notice, or perhaps you have done so already, that UFO reports are more frequent in the northern hemisphere in the warmer months of the year. Since the reports are made by people (as well as radar) they are more numerous in the spring and summer and fall because more people are out of doors and more people are glancing skyward during those months. The law of averages applies to UFOs as it does to most other things: The more people there are to look—the more will see whatever is to be seen.

As I said a while back, the summer of 1966 was replete with UFO reports. The United States had a virtual rash

103

of sightings, making 1966 a major year for the phenomena.

In the *Los Angeles Times*, August 3, 1966, Matt Weinstock reports:

"At 3 a.m. last Wednesday, July 27, three objects about 20,000 feet high and about five miles apart were seen by a group of soldiers undergoing training at Fort Gordon, Georgia.

"The reason the soldiers were up that late was that they attend classes until 2 a.m. They were returning to their barracks when they saw them.

" 'They looked like stars,' one soldier wrote to his wife, who lives in Santa Monica, 'but every fifteen seconds they would turn red and green. Every once in a while they would move up together and stop. Yesterday we heard they were UFOs. They were seen all around Fort Gordon and Augusta.' "

On the two nights preceding the sightings by the soldiers at Fort Gordon, the same or similar objects had been sighted by the control tower operators at Fulton County Airport near Atlanta.

A spokesman for the Federal Aviation Agency who was asked about the report by newsmen the next day told them that ". . . the UFOs were sighted by several people . . . reputable individuals who all work for the FAA."

In his written report to the FAA, Mr. Robert A. Bennett, the Watch Supervisor at the airport during the night, tells what happened:

"3:52 A.M. At 3:40 A.M. I stepped out the door and saw two (2) unusually bright lights close together and almost due west of the station, moving in opposite directions. I thought at first that the lights were satellites until one veered suddenly to the N.E. at increased speed, while the other continued on course for a moment or two, then became stationary. Remarked to the LSF operator for clarification that such action did not conform to an accepted satellite motion. Other observers were Mr. F. B. Self, Mrs. P. C. Graham, Mrs. Anna Lawing and Vender Steed of the Flight Service Station and John C., of Maintenance. Weather observation, clear. Visibility, 15 miles.

"4:25 A.M. While checking on cloud bank from the N.E. saw a bright light N.E. of the station. It seemed to be stationary and a look at it through the binoculars showed an oblong object, apparently reflecting the light and trailing or dangling from the bright light. Obscuring clouds prevented further observation. Sky above station was still clear, visibility 15 miles.

"4:30 A.M. Atlanta [Airport] Tower phoned to say that a Talapoosa policeman had reported moving lights with no sounds. Both tower and central radar had revealed the objects to be about 15 miles N.W. of Carrollton 'about an hour ago.' The tower said the incident had been reported to Dobbins Air Force Base.

"Report submitted [for night of July 25, 1966] by Robert A. Bennett, Watch Supervisor, Fulton County Airport, Atlanta, Georgia."

The report for the following night was also interesting:

"2:40 A.M. Phoned Atlanta [Airport] Tower to advise of UFO sighted by JBS and JC of Maintenance at 2:30. Tower unable to see object and radar unable to pick it up.

"2:45 A.M. Finished reporting UFO to Officer of the Day at Dobbins Air Force Base. Including that the object was almost due east of the station, had previously moved toward the north, then to the east, and that its appearance was that of an oval shape, vertically. Identical to the one seen 23 hours ago, including the oblong trailer which reflected the light. The OD at AFB said he would make a note of it.

"2:50 A.M. Route Traffic Control Center phoned to ask if we still had the object in sight, that they were unable to identify it on radar. [Evidently the Route Traffic Control Center had it on radar but could not tell what it was.—F.E.]

"2:55 A.M. Object had apparently become stationary and believed by some FSS observers to be a star; however, through binoculars I saw a section of the object separate and drop a short distance below the main section, then hang. J. C. of Maintenance said that the object had been subtly changing colors of red, green and blue. I could confirm this through binoculars. J. C. with the aid of binoculars confirmed that the object had separated itself.

"3:25 A.M. While I was watching the first object as it still remained stationary, JC and FBS saw another object high and to the west and moving. It moved northward and I could see through the binoculars the same subtly changing colored lights that had marked the first object. As I was comparing the two, I saw a third object near the horizon, slightly further north than the first. VDS and JC confirmed this.

"3:30 A.M. ARTCC phoned to ask if we still had the object in sight and I told the speaker of the two additional UFOs. He reported no sighting.

"3:36 A.M. On the third attempt contacted Dobbins AFB on the phone and informed the OD of the two additional UFOs. After identifying the Flight Service Station and its location the OD said 'Thank you very much,' without asking for further information.

4:05 A.M. According to Clinometer reading, the stationary object (UFO) ENE of the station was 30 degrees above the plane of the earth. While measuring I saw a second object moving from the east to the north at a greater distance than the first object from the station. The stationary UFO was about 205 degrees relative to the constella-

tion Orion. Broken clouds finally blocked view of UFO. Other witnesses to most of the above were PGG and AHL.
Report submitted by Robert A. Bennett
Watch Supervisor, Flight Service Station
Fulton County Airport, Atlanta, Georgia."

David M. Roth of Fort Wayne, Indiana, is well known as a highly successful realtor there. On July 22, 1966, his son John was coming home on leave from service in the U.S. Navy Medical Corps at Great Lakes Training Station. The father had driven to the Pennsylvania Railroad station to meet his son. It was a warm, star-bright moonless night. The two men were driving toward their summer home at Clear Lake where the family spent much of its time.

The young man was talking about his medical work, and Dave was driving along a state road in the country. It was 11:25 p.m. Dave saw something pass over the car. He did not want to interrupt the young man's conversation, so he said nothing. A minute later the same thing happened again; something made a pass just above the car top and then vanished in the darkness. Some kind of strange bird, Dave thought. A few seconds later it made the third pass . . . and he noticed that John had ceased talking.

"Did you notice anything flying over the car, John?"

With a nervous chuckle the young man replied, "Yes. Must be some kind of prehistoric bird."

Mr. Roth slowed the car to a crawl and both men stuck their heads out the windows of the car.

David Roth described it:

"It was round and saucerlike in shape, about twenty-five feet in diameter. The lower part of the craft was convex. There were portholes visible. It made absolutely no sound. It just hovered there about thirty feet above the

107

road, just above the telephone wires and only a short distance ahead of the car."

As the two men watched, the thing hung there in the air, visible in the lights of their car. The UFO swayed from side to side with a falling leaf motion, the witnesses said. Then it zoomed upward and in seconds was gone.

Numbed by their experience, the two Roths drove the remaining two miles to their cabin, but they got little sleep. Next morning they found that several other persons had seen lights hovering in the sky at the time they had had their close-up look at a UFO—an experience which neither man is anxious to repeat.

The UFOs made news again on July 27th at Winston-Salem, North Carolina (the same night they were seen at Fort Gordon, Georgia), making the third straight day that they were reported in the southeastern part of the United States by competent witnesses. On the 27th they were seen over five North Carolina towns, according to United Press. There was the customary "explanation" that the North Carolina sightings were nothing but exhausts from military jets, but the United Press adds that a Federal Aviation Agency official had reported watching UFOs.

The *Frankfort* (Indiana) *Times* reported on July 28th that residents in the southern part of Clinton County had been told that the lights they saw in the sky were nothing more than searchlights from Indianapolis. [I checked, and there were no searchlights being used in Indianapolis that night.—F.E.]

The paper adds:

"But Mrs. Larry Fish, wife of the Deputy Sheriff, had a more intimate brush with the lights.

"Mrs. Fish, who reported the incident to Deputy Huffer at the Sheriff's Office, said that she was driving down State

108

Road 28 near the junction with State Road 29 when the area around her car became brightly illuminated.

"She described a light just above the tree tops alongside the road. 'It looked like a big white puff of light,' Mrs. Fish said, 'and it lit up the road and the car and a nearby barn.'

"It also stopped her car.

"Mrs. Fish insisted that at no time did she remove her foot from the accelerator. When the light blinked off, her car was again able to move."

The newspapers and broadcasting stations around Washington, D.C., carried numerous detailed reports of eerie objects in the skies of the District of Columbia and contiguous areas on the night of July 31st. United Press reported that the Federal Aviation Agency had admitted that some of the UFOs were picked up on their numerous radar screens in the heavily traveled zone of the nation's capital. The FAA said that the only sighting reports they got that night came from police—but there were plenty of those.

City police switchboards were flooded with calls from persons wanting to report the strange things they were watching.

A group of Prince Georges County and Maryland State Patrol officers stood along the highway near Beltsville, Maryland, and watched six brightly glowing objects maneuvering in the direction of Baltimore.

They were unable to see any definite shape to the UFOs, the officers said, even with binoculars, due to the brilliant blue to green to red lights flashing from the things.

Said one of the Maryland State Patrolmen: "The things gave us goosepimples. I suggest that they not try to tell us we were merely watching swamp gas last night!"

Flying at an altitude of 9,500 feet near Sebring, Florida,

on September 20, 1966, veteran pilot James J. O'Connor suddenly discovered that he had company—strange company, at that. The time, 10:00 a.m.

O'Connor reports that he first saw the object about five hundred feet or so above his plane. He began to climb and leveled off at ten thousand feet. The UFO must have been descending, for in an estimated thirty-seven seconds it had enlarged from the size of a dollar at arm's length to the approximate size of a football field. By this time it was very close and directly above O'Connor's plane—so close that it completely shadowed the plane. He felt engulfed by the size and the sound coming from the thing. He described the noise as like that made by rubber tires screeching on a rainy pavement.

In his signed statement on the case, a copy of which is in the NICAP files, O'Connor estimated that he was in the shadow of the object for about three minutes.

"Then," he adds, "I pulled the power off my craft and put on the carburetor heat, pulled up the nose until I stalled out and dove as fast as I could without putting undue strain on the plane. I dropped to 3,500 feet before I looked up again—and that's when I became frightened—that thing had not changed size at all; it was right with me and pacing me.

"It was still as big as a football field and still right over my head. I banked to the left. It was still above me—sometimes it was beside me. . . . . . I banked to the right. Same thing. I pulled up in a power stall and peeled off. The thing was with me all that time . . . every minute."

O'Connor was so alarmed by this time that he had reached for the .38 caliber pistol he always carries in the plane. Just then he realized that the thing was changing shape. As he watched he could see that it had merely turned on edge and was climbing rapidly. In a few seconds it had climbed out of sight.

In his report on the incident the pilot says: "It was doing a reverse peel in a 360 degree turn. We don't have any aircraft that can do this, I think. It was more like the thing was falling up!"

O'Connor's feeling that the thing was "falling up" fits in with the observations of eight members of the Royal Canadian Air Force. They were refueling a plane near Summerside, on Prince Edward Island, which lies in the Atlantic north of the state of Maine. The time was 6:30 a.m., on the morning of September 21st, the day after O'Connor had his bizarre experience several thousand miles to the south.

The fliers noticed a circular, shiny object moving at very high speed, east of their base. To their astonishment it abruptly stopped, hovered a few seconds, then began to descend. When it had reached a point at which it was not more than two or three hundred feet above the ground, it again stopped, and hovered for twenty minutes.

Then, as in the case of the thing which had paced O'Connor, the object shot straight upward at fantastic speed and climbed out of sight in a matter of seconds, according to the eight military pilots who witnessed the craft.

Four days prior to the Prince Edward Island case just reported, Mr. and Mrs. Ronald MacGilvary of Crane's Beach on Ipswich Bay, Massachusetts, reported to authorities that they had watched a strange, lighted object which hovered within a few feet of the sand, while smaller glowing elliptical objects flew around it and over the surrounding terrain.

The MacGilvarys told NICAP investigator H. W. Eismann that the incident occurred at about 4:45 a.m. They describe the UFO as a thing that glowed with a golden-white light, sometimes very dim but at other times so bright that they could see the sand on the beach where it apparently had landed, just at the water's edge. The other objects, much smaller than the one that had apparently landed, approached the UFO with a skipping motion—alternately fast and slow—and seemed to settle on top of the large craft, leaving it from time to time to vanish at very low altitude behind the hills which ring the beach.

The UFO was on or near the beach for about an hour before it finally vanished around a low hill on an island about a quarter of a mile from the MacGilvary home.

The Brookline police had received two calls earlier that night of a glowing, blue-green, egg-shaped thing that was hovering over a park.

The chairman of the NICAP subcommittee in the area, Raymond Fowler, checked with the Coast Guard and was told that no planes were in the area at the time of the sightings. Mr. Fowler also verified that Venus did not rise until half an hour *after* the MacGilvary sighting and that Echo 2 had passed over that area four hours *before* the sighting.

September was studded with UFO reports from all over the country. At Eau Claire, Wisconsin, the police blotter carries the reports of police officers Carl Skamfer and Donald Brunn, who watched two strangely maneuvering objects darting about in the night sky, beginning at 9:25 p.m. The Eau Claire police had been alerted by the police in Durand that they had been watching an object with red, blue, and white flashing lights, last seen moving very slowly toward Eau Claire.

Officer Skamfer was the first to spot the thing, as he drove along Skyline Drive. He kept it in sight for about forty-five minutes. Later, Officer Brunn and a reporter for the *Eau Claire Telegram* who was with him spotted a similar object in the northeast, directly opposite the thing Skamfer was watching.

For about an hour the witnesses watched these things. Sometimes they hovered motionless for long periods of time, then they would bob up and down and dart away at tremendous speed, only to stop abruptly and zip back toward each other.

When the Eau Claire police made inquiry at the airport they were told that the objects could have been satellites— an obvious impossibility.

The *Eau Claire Telegram* said on September 8th:

"Satellites travel across the sky at tremendous speed. A few are orbited to hang above the earth but do they have flashing colored lights?

"Weather balloons sometimes reflect lights but they are blown across the sky and do not normally stay in one place —and certainly not two of them for such a long period.

"They were too high in the sky to be marsh gas and if they were helicopters they would have been too close not to hear the noise of their motors.

"What they were no one seems to know—but they were there!"

I spoke at Anderson College, about thirty miles northeast of Indianapolis, on the evening of September 20th. We had a capacity audience to hear what I had to say about UFOs and to see my pictures. That was on Tuesday.

On Saturday morning, shortly before 4:30 a.m., Henry Fox, the Security Officer at Anderson College, was driving around the campus, opening the buildings for the morning session. He was accompanied by his nine-year-old son, Darryl.

"I turned into 5th Street and there it was," the Security Officer told newsmen. "In the east I saw this perfectly round gaslike flame. It was coming toward me at terrific speed. I thought it was some sort of giant flame but when it got close enough I could see that there was something sticking out of the top of it. The thing that stuck out of the extreme top of it also protruded down into the object. Then I could see that it wasn't just some sort of gas or flame.

"By this time I was out of the car and moving around watching this thing. I shaded my eyes from the street light and I noticed that this was a solid object, for it blacked out the stars as it passed. After the blue flame effect diminished I could see that the thing was several hundred feet tall, and that it was a dull, glowing white. I was looking up at an angle of at least forty-five degrees at it—I thought it was just about over the football field at the College. I ran into the music hall to phone the police. When I came out the thing was gone.

"I called the police in Anderson to report what I had seen. They said that a similar thing had been reported by the police and Indiana State Police from Charlestown, Columbus, Shelbyville, Greensboro, Franklin, Portland and Frankfort, Ky."

Because NASA had launched a cloud of barium gas at high altitude from Wallops Island, Virginia, that same morning, the theory that it was this cloud of gas which had been sighted in Indiana was offered by way of explanation. However, that falls by the wayside when certain facts are considered. In the first place, the cloud of gas off the Atlantic coast would have been visible only slightly above the horizon, if it could have been seen at all from Indiana, which is doubtful. The glowing thing seen over Indiana was high in the sky—many of the witnesses estimated, as did Fox, that it was at least forty-five degrees above the horizon. Furthermore, there were no reports whatever from any points west of Indianapolis, therefore the object seen was at low altitude, as the witnesses estimated. And the one factor that completely rules out the "gas cloud" explanation is the simple fact that the sightings in Indiana occurred almost an hour *before* the rocket was launched from Wallops Island.

From the information furnished by scores of witnesses, it becomes apparent that they saw a huge glowing thing, moving at low altitude from north to south, on a line from Anderson, Indiana, to Frankfort, Kentucky.

Nor was that the last of such things in the area.

On Thursday, September 30th, two city policemen of Anderson were leaving the hospital cafeteria, when they spotted a glowing white object southwest of the city. Officer David Leer reported that the thing seemed to be about the size of the fuselage of a jetliner. It was moving southwest when it changed course and altitude . . . and color. The officers agreed that as the thing slowed down it changed from white to pink to red, then began "to emit a pulsating bluish-white light from underneath." Leer at first thought it might have been a satellite but ruled this out when he realized that there was a cloud cover and the thing was well below the clouds.

My personal records show sixty reports of sightings during the month of October; NICAP's files exceed that figure somewhat since they also include sightings from other countries. Something—or somebody—was very busy up there during the month of October.

Near Temple, Oklahoma, on October 3rd, mysterious pulsating red lights were reported flying about at very low altitude, estimated by motorists at not more than sixty feet above the road. City Marshal Howard Douglas also reported being among those who witnessed the strange, silent lights, four in number, which the officer estimated were not more than twenty-five feet above the ground when he saw them.

At Polson, Montana, the night watchman at the Plum Creek Lumber Company and Kalispell police both reported a glowing bluish-white thing that was moving south to north at 1:40 a.m. First guess that it was a meteor had to be discarded because of the length of time it was in view.

At about 5 o'clock on the morning of October 3rd, witnesses in Gulfport, Mississippi, and in Harvey and Gentilly, suburbs of New Orleans, reported watching a UFO. The sightings began a few minutes before 5 a.m. and ended about 5:45 when a blimplike thing with rows of lights along the bottom and top was first reported near Gulfport, moving westward in the general direction of New Orleans. At 5:15 a.m. four persons in one group reported watching such a craft near Gentilly and two plant guards and several other persons reported a football- or oval-shaped thing in the sky bearing two rows of lights, and apparently hovering for several minutes.

Both the International and Lakefront Airports assured newsmen who made inquiry that they knew of no blimps in the area.

At Taree, Australia, a cigar-shaped UFO with a row of lighted windows or portholes along the side was reported on the night of Monday, October 2nd. The five witnesses told authorities they had the thing in view for about fifteen minutes and that it flew silently, on an erratic course, frequently pausing for a few seconds in flight. It was similar to an object reported the previous week from the Yarras district, the *Sydney Herald* reported.

Paragould, Arkansas, apparently had a UFO sighting on the early evening of October 7th, when a lady called the office of the *Daily Press* to alert them to a strange light in the sky to the north of the city. Don Fletcher, a reporter for the paper, was among those who joined some other staff members and numerous residents of Paragould in the parking lot behind the paper, where they reportedly had a good look at a bright object, moving northward at a pace which they described as jerky but very fast. While watching this performance, the witnesses detected two more UFOs moving eastward, much slower than the northbound object. "They appear to jump and move in a kind of circular orbit," says the *Paragould Press,* which speculates that they might have been balloons at very high altitude. (The circular orbit would rule out the balloon theory, since balloons would be at the mercy of the wind—and wind does not blow in circles at high altitude.—F.E.)

Wanaque Reservoir, near Paterson, New Jersey, was again the scene of UFO action in October, after its interesting case of the preceding January.

The October incident opened when a lady called the Pompton Lakes police from her home on a mountain top near Fayette Lakes to report that a glistening UFO had passed between her home and the cable-television tower nearby, which is about five hundred feet tall.

The Pompton Lakes police broadcast the alert that a strange object had been reported in the area . . . and by 9:25 p.m. sighting reports were pouring in from a line between Pompton Lakes and Wanaque Reservoir. Most of them reported a glowing white object at very low altitude, moving silently from point to point.

At Wanaque, the witnesses phoned the reservoir guards to report that something had been maneuvering around the dam and seemed to have landed in the reservoir. Police Sergeant Ben Thompson, who went to the dam to investigate the reports, radioed back to headquarters that he was watching a brightly glowing object "—the size of an automobile—" and that it was hovering over the dam at not more than one hundred fifty feet altitude.

Said Sergeant Thompson: "It's lighting up practically the whole southern end of the reservoir!"

Thompson turned on the flashing red light on the top of his patrol car and the UFO blacked out and vanished from the area. However, it was seen a few seconds later by Patrolman William Pastor, from the headquarters of the reservoir police.

Pastor reported that the object would pause for a few seconds from time to time as it moved in a northerly direction at an altitude of three or four hundred feet. When last seen it was over the upper end of the reservoir, moving toward New York State.

Pastor told newsmen that he had seen the same or a similar object several times before but that this was the closest he had been to it. He added that the Air Force had sent a team to the reservoir after the January, 1966, sighting and that the Air Force team had taken pictures of the object.

The Air Force withdrew its original explanation of the January UFO at Wanaque ("a brightly lighted helicopter") and declined comment on what it or the one in October might have been.

118

(It might be noted that in the Wanaque cases the official explainers were applying a technique which they have found very useful, especially in cases where the witnesses are of a caliber that would be awkward or unwise to refute. Newsmen who made inquiry about the second Wanaque case in October were told that the Air Force had not been "officially notified" and therefore had no comment!)

Frank Delle, Jr., President of radio station WLKN in Lincoln, Maine, tells me that one night in October of 1966 he was called out of a meeting by an individual who reported that something was hovering over the station's transmitting tower. By the time he arrived on the scene, says Mr. Delle, the normally deserted road was jammed with cars. Four portable telescopes had been set up. Most of the objects the observers watched were stars, but two of them definitely were not stars. These moved steadily from east to west, which no manmade satellite does, and glowed with a steady red light. They were positively not planes or balloons, Mr. Delle says the Air Force assured him.

(He adds that his station carries my daily radio program "Flying Saucers—Serious Business," and that the high school has advised its history students to listen to the program every day, if possible.—F.E.)

The family of Abram (Bud) Lodder, of Union Valley Road near West Milford, New Jersey, had been watching some odd things in the night sky, but they told authorities that they were reluctant to mention what they had seen until the Wanaque case in October made front pages.

The Lodders told authorities that they had seen oval-shaped lights bobbing around in the vicinity of their home, which is several miles from the scene of the Wanaque sighting. When the objects were near their home, said the Lodders, the static on both their radio and television was so

119

bad that neither device was usable. As soon as the UFOs had gone away the sets were in perfect operating condition again.

Near the Lodders there is a fire tower about a thousand feet high (above sea level) and it was around this tower that the Lodders saw the oval-shaped lights bobbing. They were in sight about ten minutes on each occasion, according to the witnesses. Mr. Lodder told authorities, "The things were shaped like an egg and the light they gave off was as bright as a welder's arc!"

Walter Stone of Rural Route 3, Carlisle, Kentucky, reported to police an experience which is similar to numerous others under similar conditions.

On the morning of October 18, 1966, Mr. Stone reported that he was driving to work at the Kawneer Company plant in Cynthiana. The time, 5:55 a.m.

Stone told Police Chief Edgar Navarre that, as he topped a hill on Kentucky Highway 36, about two miles east of Cynthiana, his car lights flashed on the UFO. The object shot over the car at a high rate of speed. Said Stone, "I heard a whine from it and it hurt my ears!" He told the police that the bottom of the top-shaped object was covered with a white light or whitish flames . . . and that there was a ring of red light or flames around the outer edge.

"It scared me," said Stone. "I'm all shook up and I hope I don't see it no more!"

By this time the government—especially the Defense Department—was "all shook up" also, and had made a contract with the University of Colorado for a small group of scientists there, under the direction of Professor Edward U. Condon, to undertake a limited ($313,000) study of

UFOs from a scientific standpoint. The study, according to a statement from the office of Secretary of the Air Force Harold Brown, was to be ". . . independently of and without direction from the Air Force." As I reported to you earlier in this book, the Air Force evidently didn't get the message and had to modify its original statement that the study would be based on "selected material from Air Force files."

Just what it will amount to will depend on what it *is* based on, which is why I am keeping my fingers crossed and hoping for the best, which will be a pleasant surprise if that's what it turns out to be.

October not only produced the wedding of the Colorado scientists and the Blue Bookers, it also brought a rare and interesting disclosure: Our military space-scanning equipment had been tracking three "unknowns" orbiting Earth!

Although the Air Force has categorically denied that any UFOs have ever been tracked by radar—North American Air Defense Command (NORAD) exploded the statement with its official admission that it had been tracking not one, but *three* unknowns for more than a month. The existence of the objects was confirmed in the Satellite Situation Report from the Goddard Space Flight Center.

Aviation Week magazine said that two of the objects were too small to be detected by the Naval Space Surveillance System, which did detect a six-inch-long piece of metal in orbit. But there seems to be some difference of opinion on that score, for the *World Journal Tribune* of New York City quotes the official spokesman for 9th Aerospace Defense Division of the Air Force Center at Colorado Springs as saying, on October 28th:

"We have not listed them as debris and we have no

121

problem tracking them. We assume they are debris. We don't know how long they have been aloft, or their source, or their size."

A check with France and Britain and a re-examination of all the Soviet launchings revealed nothing that could account for the objects. Two of the things were in polar orbits. The third object, orbiting at an angle of about 35 degrees from the equator is officially catalogued as No. 2428, *and it is about the size of Telstar* according to official determination.

Please note that NORAD admits that this "unknown" was first discovered in orbit in March of 1966. Two months later, on CBS-TV on May 10th, it was asserted that no unknowns had ever been detected by our tracking gear.

Autumn of 1966 saw a couple of interesting actions other than the revelation by NORAD which we have just detailed. It was on September 19th that the Air Force issued a new order on UFO procedure, superseding its long-standing AFR 200-2.

That (AFR 200-2) was the order under which the Air Force established its own procedures for carrying out the investigative duties re UFOs which were assigned to it by JANAP 146, back in 1952. AFR 200-2 established the rules of procedure which had to be followed in dealing with the UFO problem. AFR 200-2 also reminded all Air Force personnel of the severe penalties awaiting anyone who violated its provisions by making public statements without approval.

AFR 200-2 was superseded on September 19, 1966, by AFR 80-17, which merely transferred the UFO probe from Intelligence to Research and Development. This was presumably a move to prepare a more nearly equal mental level between the Air Force UFO probers and the scientists in other agencies and outside the government, with whom they would be working.

You will note that this change was made in mid-September and the contract with the Condon group at the University of Colorado went into effect shortly thereafter.

There is nothing really new in AFR 80-17, but a couple of paragraphs are interesting. Under Paragraph 12, "Reporting Physical Evidence," Item No. 5 says: "RADAR. Forward two copies of each still camera photographic print. Title radarscope prints per AFR 95-7. Classify radarscope photographs per AFR 205-1."

This means that radar picks up UFOs and they are photographed from the radar screen. It also means that radar sightings of UFOs are *automatically classified and may not be discussed or revealed to the public.*

Then again, in that same Paragraph 12, Item b:

"Air Force echelons receiving suspected or *actual* UFO material will safeguard it to prevent any defacing or alterations which might reduce its value for Intelligence examination and analysis." (Italics mine.—F.E.)

This order preceded the beginning of operations with the Condon Committee. Immediately following that important step, AFR 80-17 was modified, on November 8th by the issuance of AFR 80-17A, which ordered that ALL UFO reports must be sent to the University of Colorado (Condon Committee) . . . with this interesting exception. . . . "Every effort will be made to keep all UFO reports unclassified. However, if it is necessary to classify a report because of a method of detection or other factors not related to the UFO, a separate report *including all possible information* will be sent to the University of Colorado." (Italics mine.—F.E.)

As a veteran newsman with many years of dealing with

123

the military, I cannot construe that as other than an escape hatch, through which important UFO cases may be withheld and, in their stead, denatured or "edited" reports submitted, if that seems preferable to the censors in the military hierarchy.

On November 17th, a truck driver phoned the Sinton, Texas, police station at 4:11 a.m. He reported that a flashing bright light had paced his truck all the way from Victoria, at one time dropping to within two hundred feet of the ground. When Police Officer Pete Anzaldua went to the truck stop from which the man had phoned, he found a badly shaken big man who could hardly drink his coffee. The truck driver took a group, including the policeman, outside and pointed out the light that he referred to. Officer Anzaldua said: "It looked like a rotary light on top of a police car. It was like a ball with three different colored lights. Once in a while it would shine like a ray of the sun, like lightning. It was about the size of a softball at fifty feet. Sometimes it would go lower. The lights continually went on and off."

Presently the light began to move toward Odem. The police officer went back to headquarters and reported it to Dispatcher Gene Norton, who watched it for a few minutes and called Sheriff's Deputy Bobby Horn at Odem. Horn observed the thing through binoculars for more than an hour. During that time it again moved toward the north, finally moving to the southeast and rising as it did so. The police told newsmen that the object was still visible after dawn, and was rising when last seen.

Three days later came the official explanation: They had all been watching the planet Venus, according to officials at the Naval Air Station and the Corpus Christi Weather Bureau. Venus, they said, "—seen under abnormally clear weather conditions," etc. All they had to do to arrive at that conclusion was to ignore about half the known facts in the case, as reported by credible witnesses.

Said the *Corpus Christi Caller-Times*:

"However, police who observed the object were not convinced by the explanation."

Amen.

Vincent Perna, a 23-year-old construction worker from Yonkers, N.Y., was fishing with his brother and another friend in Lake Tiorati. This is a long finger-shaped reservoir about 35 miles north of Times Square, on the west side of the Hudson river, near Pearl River, New York. The date was December 18th, 1966. The time, shortly after 4:30 p.m.

In the report made to authorities after the incident, Perna said that he glanced up and noticed an unusual object which had apparently come from behind Fingerboard Mountain. The three men saw it fly over the fire tower at Tiorati, then it maneuvered briefly over the lake near the point at which they were fishing.

Perna had a small, plastic Brownie Starflash camera. It was a simple form of box camera, loaded with black and white film. Perna dug the camera out of his tackle box and managed to make four snaps before the object sped away over Stockbridge Mountain.

The three witnesses described the object as a dull copper-colored thing, 15 to 18 feet from rim to rim and slightly less than that in height. It was silent in operation and accelerated with remarkable speed.

Perna and his two companions hurried to inform the park patrol officers of what had happened. At the officers' suggestion, they called Stewart Air Force base and made a report. The officer who took the call advised Perna to send the negative and any prints they might have to the base for examination.

[The negatives were sent, as per instructions, and amazingly, Perna actually got them back with a letter stating that the object had been determined to be of 3-4 feet in diameter. This is an interesting conclusion, since it contradicts previous Air Force statements in other sightings, where the Air Force has correctly pointed out that it is impossible to compute the size of an object without knowing its distance from the camera. In the Perna case, that distance was unknown.—F.E.]

The incident was also reported to the *Rockland* (New York) *News,* which in turn contacted the Stewart Air Force Base. The paper found that Perna had indeed reported the incident, as he claimed, and that the officer who discussed the matter with the paper, one Lieutenant Gerald Custin, told the paper that the object on Perna's negatives was nothing more than a "blob of developing fluid." But the newspaper had the prints, which they had examined and concluded were genuine, and they continued to question Lt. Custin, who admitted that he had not even seen the negatives which he was attempting to evaluate!

The *Rockland News* carried the pictures and the story on the front page of their issue for December 29, 1966.

(See picture section for copies of the Perna pictures.)

Frank J. Carleglio, chairman of the NICAP Subcommittee at Emerson, New Jersey, opened the investigation for that organization. He obtained the negatives taken by Perna for examination by photographic experts working with NICAP, and he arranged for Perna to be questioned by Dr. Charles T. Henderson, a psychiatrist of New York City.

Two teams of photographic experts reported to NICAP that in their opinions the photos taken by Perna had been taken as claimed, and were therefore valid pictures of an Unidentified Flying Object.

Dr. Henderson, who interrogated Perna at length while Perna was under the effects of sodium pentothal ("truth serum"), pronounced Perna's account of the incident, in his opinion, to be a correct account of what had actually happened.

In May of 1967, the Condon Committee at the University of Colorado asked for and received the Perna negatives for examination. They have announced no conclusions on the pictures as I write this, in late June.

Because of the apparent authenticity of the pictures, they could conceivably become among the most important civilian UFO photos ever taken.

4/21/67—South Hill, Va. William Powers, Northwestern University engineer and assistant to Dr. J. Allen Hynek, UFO investigator for the Air Force, examines scorched road surface with witness R. N. Crowder, warehouse manager who said he saw tubular UFO take-off in front of his car.

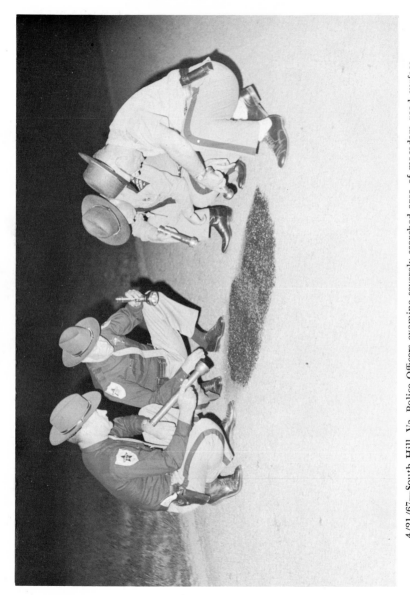

4/21/67—South Hill, Va. Police Officers examine severely scorched area of macadam road surface where UFO take-off was observed by credible local resident.

4/21/67—South Hill, Va. Site of UFO landing on macadam road surface. Insets show some of four tiny holes arranged in a rectangle around a scorched area on the road surface. Spectators indicate positions of holes.

12/18/66—Lake Tiorati, N.Y. One of two exposures of a UFO taken by Yonkers resident Vincent Perna, with other witnesses. After careful investigation, NICAP had found no flaws in the photos or story as of July 1967.

12/18/66—Lake Tiorati (enlargement).

8/8/65—Santa Ana, Calif. Little publicized photo of UFO by Rex Heflin, county highway investigator. UFO banked across highway; two-way radio in county vehicle failed as UFO passed.

134

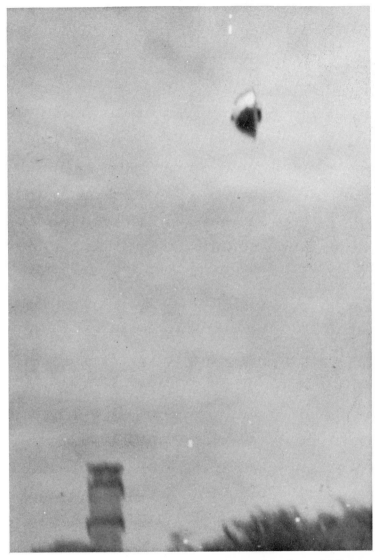

4/2/66—Melbourne, Victoria, Australia. Photo taken by a Melbourne businessman from his garden. Original is in color. Case is under investigation by NICAP and APRO.

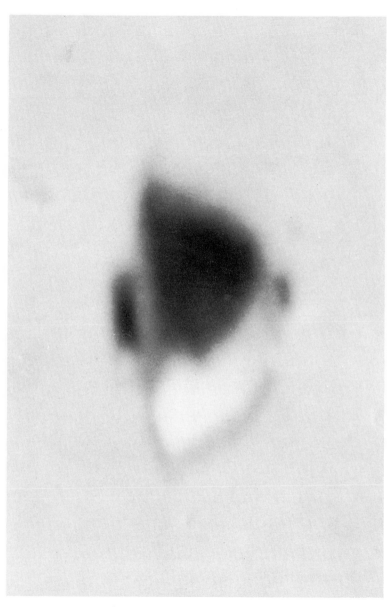

4/2/66—Melbourne (enlargement).

"But you don't understand! I haven't even seen Europe yet!"

7

Each year adds a new name or two to the list of those who claim to have been contacted by the operators of the UFOs. In 1966 the names of Mr. and Mrs. Barney Hill were added to the list. And thanks to their story being reported in *Look* magazine, they got more attention than some of their recent predecessors.

Persons who tell such stories are known in the UFO business as "contactees."

The first and foremost among them was a fellow named George Adamski. He was a man of meager scholastic attainments, but he made up for that shortcoming by having an excellent imagination, a pleasing personality, and an apparently endless supply of gall.

George established the ground rules for the contactees which they have dutifully followed. He was the first—and he showed that there was considerable loot to be made by peddling tales of talking with space people. George instinctively realized that everything had to be pretty nebulous; he knew that details would be disastrous.

Prior to becoming associated with a hamburger stand on the road to Mt. Palomar, George had worked in a hamburger stand as a grill cook. With this scientific background he wrote, in his spare time, a document which he called *An Imaginary Trip to the Moon, Venus and Mars.* He voluntarily listed it with the Library of Congress for copyright purposes as *a work of fiction.*

139

That was in 1949.

His effort did not attract many customers but it did attract the attention of a lady writer who saw gold in them there space ships. She made a deal with George to rewrite his epic; she was to furnish the skilled writing and he was to furnish the photographs of the space ships.

This lady brought the finished manuscript to me for appraisal and she brought with it a clutch of the crudest UFO photographs I had seen in years. I declined to have anything to do with the mess and she left my office in a bit of a huff.

In its revised form it told a yarn of how George had ventured into the desert of southern California, where he met a "scout ship" from which stepped a gorgeous doll in golden coveralls. She spoke to him with a bell-like voice in a language which he did not understand, so they had to resort to telepathy, or something similar, to carry on their conversation. And then, as she prepared to leave him, she tapped out a message in the sand with her little boot. George realized that she wanted him to preserve this message (it was terribly important) and, having a pocket full of wet plaster of Paris (which he seemingly always carried with him on desert trips), George quickly made a plaster cast of the footprint with the message, which he eventually reproduced for the educational advancement of his readers, who were legion.

Of the numerous photographs which embellished the book let it be said that some of them could not have been taken as claimed. The others were crudely "simulated," as the Air Force put it charitably.

But for me the payoff was the alleged photograph of Adamski's "scout ship" in which he allegedly took a trip to Venus and returned. The picture as shown in his book was taken either on a day when three suns were shining—or else it was a small object taken with three floodlights for illumination. After eight years of patient search I finally came to the conclusion that his space ship was in reality the top of a cannister-type vacuum cleaner, made in 1937. I doubt that many persons are traveling through space in vacuum cleaner tops.

Adamski communicated with me frequently. When he was questioned about the title of "professor" which he used, he explained that it was just an honorary title given to him by his "students," and that he never used it himself. George was evidently forgetful, for the letters he sent to me were always signed "Professor George Adamski."

But this congenial con man sold a jillion books to those who were eager to believe that somebody from space was crossing millions of miles of the trackless void for the dubious privilege of conversing telepathically with former hamburger cooks. Adamski toured this country on the lecture circuit; then he branched out into Europe, where he even arranged a private confab with the Queen of The Netherlands, a maneuver which stirred up quite a bit of comment for the Queen, very little of which was favorable.

The bogus professor followed his first book with another volume but it did not meet with the ready acceptance which the public had granted his first offering. For one thing, some of his "witnesses" to his alleged meeting with the golden girl from a distant galaxy had changed their minds about both George and his story. And perhaps more importantly, several other contactees had rushed into print with yarns of having ridden in space ships and of having conversed with the operators thereof.

George Adamski died in 1963 of a heart attack. At the

time of his death he was offering to teach people how to visit the planets Venus and Mars by self-hypnosis . . . for fifty dollars.

George the First has had many imitators down through the years. By and large they have followed the lessons laid down by their successful pioneer: Keep your stories devoid of details. Deal in generalities. Have the meetings with the space people take place in the most isolated places possible. No witnesses. (Look what happened to Adamski and his "witnesses"!)

Even Adamski had a predecessor in this field of specious space travel. There was the Denton family of New England, a family of oddballs who flourished around the latter part of the preceding century. The father was a hypnotist who could, and did, put his wife and two sons into a trance state. While they were thus becalmed he would hand one of them a rock and tell them that it was from either Mars or Jupiter or the moon. Then he would tell the one holding the pebble that he wanted him to go to that planet and tell what he saw there.

Needless to say, their reports were short on detail but full of imagination and glowing generalities, remarkably similar to those of the contactees of our own generation. Perhaps it is from Mr. Denton's orders that his subjects make the trip in hypnotic trance that George Adamski got his idea of selling instructions on "how to travel through space under hypnosis."

Among Adamski's numerous carbon copies was one fellow who professed to be meeting with the space people in a big ditch behind his home. According to this professional-sign-painter-turned-space-authority, the occupants of the UFOs would drift down silently into a deep ravine in his orchard. They would then summon him (by telepathy) to come and confer with them about world problems and how to meet them.

According to his account of these meetings, the space people were very much concerned about Man and the danger of our blowing ourselves to bits with runaway nuclear explosions. This had happened before in our solar system, so he said, and it was pretty messy for those quiet-loving characters on the other planets.

Among other things, the space people confided in him how they lived and what they ate, and he says they gave him some of their favorite recipes. Again, nothing in writing—just some information which they had him memorize. He, in turn, passed this information along to his wife, and after she had memorized it thoroughly he sent her out among their friends and neighbors (at three days for fifty dollars) to teach those lucky ladies how to prepare food for the space visitors when they arrived—an event which he said was imminent.

One of the favorite ingredients of the space menu was ordinary broccoli chopped fine and seasoned with crushed garlic and bits of chopped onion. This was to be served on a leaf of lettuce, garnished with maraschino cherries, and served cold. If that is what the space people are eating, perhaps it explains why they are reluctant to have anyone get near them.

In England a fellow cropped up with what he said was a picture of a space man. Seems that the Englishman just remembered to take the picture as the spaceman turned to hurry back to his craft. The photograph shows a tall slender man clad in what appears to be a suit of black diver's underwear, wearing a belt around the midriff with a pair of pliers hanging over one hip. No picture of the alleged craft, no view of the man's face which might serve for identification purposes . . . just the usual windy story and the usual meaningless picture.

From Europe come two photographs of a small manlike creature standing beside a double-convex disc-shaped thing. It was assertedly taken when the craft landed in the snow near a mountain top, where the photographer just happened to be. . . . .etc.

The picture is an obvious phoney. It is unmistakably a tabletop picture of small objects arranged by hand. The evidence in support of that statement is readily understood by any trained photographer . . . but the pictures have sold all over the world to those who do not know what is wrong with them . . . or to those who do not care.

One of the most entertaining stories of alleged contact comes from a most unlikely source—a semi-literate farmer who operates a flinty farm in the Midwest.

This character vanished from his farm for about two weeks. The story that our hero told upon his return is one that he has told a great many times since, with variations.

He told his wife that he had been snatched right out of his tobacco field by a flying saucer. Never even had time to leave a note for his wife. Had to git and go, right then, or miss the trip. Naturally, he went.

Seems that he was aboard a space ship which was based on a secret planet hidden behind our sun. Now I think we will have to admit that if anyone wanted to hide a planet —he could hardly do better than that.

These space travelers didn't talk much to him. Didn't even tell him how they happened to select him—a poor tobacco farmer—out of all the people on Earth, to make this historic trip. Just fed him and told him that he would be returned to Earth after their mission was completed.

After a short and very pleasant stay on the Hidden Planet, which nobody would name for him, he expressed a desire to visit Mars. As long as he had a free ride around the solar system he wanted to make the most of it. After considerable deliberation among themselves, the spacecraft operators agreed to take him to Mars, but only for three Martian days, for it seems that they did not like either the planet or its people.

Everybody was happy on Mars, he told his wife. Everybody was singing and dancing and life was just a big endless Elk's picnic. The head of this perpetual jamboree was a little fat king, who seems to have taken a liking to our peripatetic farmer, for the king gave him a Martian dog to take home with him as a memento of his visit to Mars.

Sure enough, he had brought home with him a big fat woolly black dog—which was losing its hair. When his wife called attention to the fact that the dog's hair was falling out, our hero had the explanation.

It seems that the spacecraft people who were driving him around on this free interplanetary hayride did not like Mars, and they were allergic to Martian dogs, especially big, fat, woolly, black Martian dogs. As soon as they got well out into space on their way back to Earth, they ruled that the dog could not ride inside the spacecraft—it had to ride on the outside. And everyone knows what those cosmic rays do to a fat woolly dog riding on the outside of a flying saucer! Just cooked the hair right off that dog, that's what!

Seems that our space-traveling rustic had thoughtfully memorized the formula for making Martian dog food.

145

But when he had his wife prepare a batch of the mixture that evening the dog didn't seem to recognize it. Two days later, however, they made a wonderful discovery—the dog would eat Earth-type dog food and seemed to enjoy it.

Mom was so impressed by the story spun by her errant spouse that she decided it was too good to keep to themselves; others must hear of it too. So she began booking her interplanetary papa and his extraterrestrial dog wherever they could get a crowd together: PTA meetings, fish fries, church basement socials—just anywhere. And when he forgot and deviated from the story as he had first told it, Mom was on her feet, yelling at him and setting him straight on his own story.

What has become of them I do not know; last time I saw their show was three or four years ago. The dog was getting his hair back, their story had improved in the telling, and the two of them had a pretty good act worked out.

Illiterate though he may have been, the hero of this contactee case had heeded all the rules: He had arranged the "meeting" in a remote spot; he was pretty vague on details; and the space people were "only trying to help us."

But the contact stories of this past year have taken a more purposeful turn. Now, it seems, the space people are not all a bunch of intergalactic dogooders. There is another element among them with other interests than keeping us from blowing ourselves up.

SEX has reared its interplanetary head . . . if we are to believe this new crop of contactees.

One such story came from Brazil, where a 23-year-old farmer claims that he was taken right off his tractor by the tiny occupants of a strange craft which came down in a plowed field. The object, he told authorities, was torpedo-

146

shaped and glowing red until it settled on the ground. Then the red went out and it became a dull grey.

The creatures who got out of it were small, manlike beings dressed in striped grey suits and they had tubes on their helmets, which ran from front to back.

After escorting our young Brazilian farmer inside the craft his captors bathed him in a clear thick liquid. Then, he says, they drew off blood from two tubes inserted into his chin. When he became nauseated by this act, he was placed on a bed in a room where a greyish vapor seeped in through a maze of tiny holes in the wall.

There, he claims, he was seduced by a short blonde woman—in fact she seduced him *twice*. The most notable features of this woman were her mouth—just a narrow slit without lips—and her voice—guttural and growling.

After having concluded the *double* seduction, he says he was given his clothes, taken on a tour of the craft, and he adds that he tried to steal a small box for evidence of his experience, but his captors made him put it back.

So—all he had were his memories, a couple of small bruises on his chin, and his story about being seduced (*twice*) by a short growling blonde without lips.

But for sheer unadulterated shock we must award the pennant to this headline from the front page of the *New York Chronicle,* November 21, 1966:

I WAS RAPED IN A FLYING SAUCER

The young lady who reports this unique experience is a resident of Melbourne, Australia, Miss Marlene Travers, age 24.

Miss Travers told the reporter:

147

"Believe it or not, I was held captive in a flying saucer, raped and made pregnant by a man from outer space!"

And how did this happen? Miss Travers said that it took place while she was visiting some friends in the country. On the night of August 11th, they had been talking about flying saucers, and her friends said they had seen one a few nights previously but Miss Travers laughed and told them that living in the country had made superstitious hicks of them.

"I am a practical girl, you see—science fiction has always left me cold," she told the reporter. "Anyhow after supper I volunteered to walk a half mile down to a little crossroads store for some cigarettes. That was when it all happened —so quickly that I didn't have time to think—or anything!

"I was about halfway there when I heard a strange humming sound and saw a weird light in the sky. The sound was getting louder. At first I thought it was an airplane but it just kept getting louder and louder and then all of a sudden it landed—right there in the field—not more than thirty feet from me. It was a silvery disc about fifty feet across and about ten feet thick. It seemed to shine there in the dusk—to glow with a light of its own.

"From what my friends had told me I recognized it instantly as a spacecraft from some world other than our own.

"A sliding door opened and a man—a tall handsome man, wearing a sort of loose-fitting metallic green tunic— stepped out. He stared at me with eyes that seemed to give off light rays. I wanted to run. I wanted to scream—but I was petrified.

"He opened his mouth and although he didn't say a word —just made a kind of high-pitched whine—I understood what he was saying. It must have been a kind of telepathy

—as though he was planting his thoughts right in my mind!"

Marlene says that the tall handsome space man did not use force. When he touched her she felt compelled to obey. They entered the flying saucer, passing an instrument panel to a room which she describes as wildly furnished . . . with a remarkable faculty of getting out of focus.

Before raping her, Marlene says that the space man told her that she had been selected for an honor—that of being the first woman on Earth to bear a child by a man from his planet.

As he was leading her out of the saucer after the seduction, Marlene says she tripped some kind of switch and the resultant flash burned her ankles. Then she passed out.

When she awakened she was lying in the field where the alleged UFO had landed. She ran to the home of her friends, who had searched for her in vain, and was told that she had been missing seven hours. They called a doctor, who examined her and found burns on her legs and ankles. At the point where she claimed to have been assaulted her friends found a large indentation in the earth.

Later, Marlene Travers was again examined by a doctor, who said that she was definitely pregnant. Miss Travers is said to be convinced that when she gives birth it will be a baby from out of this world.

A 23-year-old farm boy in Brazil—and a 24-year-old girl in Australia. When will this interplanetary sex madness end? What will Ann Landers say about this?

All of which brings us to the latest of these contactees— Mr. and Mrs. Barney Hill, of Portsmouth, New Hampshire. Mr. Hill, a Negro, is a leader in NAACP activities in his community. His wife, Betty, a white woman, works for a division of Social Welfare in the state of New Hampshire.

They tell a story of having been taken aboard an Unidentified Flying Object which overtook their car along State Road 3 near Franconia Notch, New Hampshire.

As is customary with such stories, they were in an isolated area (no witnesses). It was all done in the darkness (lack of detail).

According to their story, they were taken into a huge UFO. There they were stripped and subjected to a thorough physical examination, as they told the story later, and the space people seemed to be amazed that Barney wore false teeth. Then they are alleged to have asked such penetrating questions as "What is aging?" and "What is time?" and to have inserted a needle into Mrs. Hill's navel "to see if she was pregnant."

The Hills kept mum about their alleged experience for four years, so they say. Then they appeared before a UFO group in Quincy and from there on the publicity picked up rapidly.

Eventually they were examined by a psychiatrist, Dr. Benjamin Simon, who teaches at Tufts University Medical School.

Under hypnosis, the Hills recounted their bizarre yarn of having been kidnapped. But statements made in hypnotic trance, are, as Dr. Simon says, ". . . only the road to truth as the subject sees it. In many cases this is also the objective truth—but *not always*.

"Sometimes it is not the same as the impersonal truth: what actually happened."

[In reality, it is surprisingly easy to fake a story for retelling under hypnotic trance. To accomplish this a person

150

is hypnotized and told a story while in trance. Later, when that person is again hypnotized, if questioned about the subject he will recount the story which was previously told to him. For this reason, testimony of persons given under hypnosis is regarded as unreliable.—F.E.]

What conclusions did the psychiatrist arrive at after his lengthy questioning of the Hills?

"Their case is very interesting and very complex," says Dr. Simon. "There is no way of proving that they were abducted by a UFO or that they were not abducted. *I don't believe that they were,* but the Hills do."

The widely publicized story told by the Hills becomes another unsupported and unsupportable "contact" story to add to the long list of such tales. It has all the familiar elements of such stories—and all the familiar shortcomings. Lacking proof, it must be filed along with the other followers in the steps of George Adamski as "interesting if true."

One of the lesser known figures in the contactee field is a fellow who claims to have been picked up by a UFO and flown from a desert in the southwest to New York City and back in something like eight minutes.

His alleged trip, like that of the farmer who went to the planet "hidden behind the sun," demonstrates the fantastic performance of these UFOs.

When the contactees are aboard, they travel at the speed of lie.

"They probably don't realize some mushrooms are deadly."

8

Inevitably, in an arena where so many scenes are being enacted, there must be some that excite wonder because they are included at all. Not being important to the theme of the production, by their very ineptitude they add an element of falsity and a note of confusion.

Thus it was when, on May 10th the Columbia Broadcasting System turned its television facilities over to a widely advertised "documentary" entitled "Flying Saucers: Friend, Foe or Fantasy?", it was announced as a presentation of the CBS News Department.

As a documentary it was sorely lacking in objectivity. If the material was not supplied by the Pentagon it must have been taken from old Project Blue Book handouts. It consisted of the usual half-truths and outright falsehoods which have characterized the official statements on UFOs for so many years. And there was no visible or audible attempt to challenge the perpetrators.

Several of the more flagrant deviations from fact could easily have been shown for what they were had CBS sought the services of anyone familiar with the story. But no such provision had been made.

For instance, one character made the bald assertion that "UFOs are not tracked on radar." That hoary fraud is so preposterous that selecting the reply to it is hampered by

155

the vast number of cases in which UFOs have been tracked on radar. Perhaps the most damning answer is that to be found in an official government publication—Technical Publication No. 180 of the Civil Aeronautics Administration (now the Federal Aviation Agency) —which is a booklet dealing entirely with radar tracking of UFOs. Actually the cases of confirmed radar tracking of UFO's are so numerous that selecting one as more outstanding than another is difficult. The point is that the statement, as presented on the CBS program on this subject, was demonstrably untrue.

Another debatable statement offered as evidence that UFOs are nonexistent was: "If they fly at speeds of thousands of miles per hour—why don't they ever create sonic booms?"

That is an excellent question. In fact, it is such a good question that the military is spending a great deal of time and money and manpower trying to find the answer to it. But because we cannot do it does not mean that it isn't being done. On the contrary, we know that it *is* being done, by the UFOs, even though *we* cannot *do* it. This was not explained on the program and the effect was to leave the uninformed viewer with the impression that since we could not fly faster than sound without creating sonic booms— then it couldn't be done—which was incorrect.

The third basic boner in the CBS program on UFOs was the showing of the films taken by Mrs. Thomas Oldfield over England from an airliner (reported in Chapter Four). As explained previously, the official explanation that the object she photographed was a *reflection* of the tail surfaces of the plane on the cabin window was an impossibility under the conditions. Yet whoever arranged the show for CBS included the impossible "explanation" as though it were proved fact.

The CBS "documentary" on UFOs brought a barrage of critical comment from the press, including this from Bob Mackenzie of the *Oakland* (California) *Tribune.*

Making it plain that he was no "believer" in UFOs himself, Mackenzie wrote:

"CBS's pretense of being objective was transparent and pretty annoying. Walter Kronkite's patronizing smile was two shades this side of a sneer, and the filmed evidence was carefully handpicked to foster the 'fantasy' point of view.

"CBS interviewed, primarily, two kinds of people; educated experts who do not believe in UFOs and a motley assortment of juveniles, farmers and crackpots who do believe in them . . . Military personnel, commercial airline pilots, law enforcement officers and radar trackers have reported sightings. Why weren't some of these credible observers interviewed?

"CBS showed three films of saucers in flight. Two were obviously fakes; one resulted from an optical illusion. But there are films in existence showing UFOs in formation that still have not been satisfactorily explained away. These films were undoubtedly available to CBS, which smugly declined to show them.

"I simply feel that 650 unexplained sightings are a lot of unexplained sightings, enough to make a sensible person suspect that there may be something up there. I believe that the average person knows marsh gas from molasses, and that there is no reason to classify all saucer-sighters as fibbers or fools, particularly if they have technical knowledge to back up their judgment.

"CBS interviewed a collection of quacks and characters who infest the saucer movement . . . including a lady who takes regular trips to Venus. CBS may have felt that there was some entertainment value in displaying these gifted

157

folk, but their relevance to the controversy was questionable, to say the least.

"The other side of the case got some attention. Donald Keyhoe, a retired Marine major who is in apparent control of his mental faculties, stated his belief that '. . . we are being observed by a highly advanced civilization'. . . . But the pilots and other knowledgeable witnesses who have seen UFOs were significantly absent . . . CBS did not knock itself out to keep an open mind."

Commenting on this expression NICAP said:

"From the number of similar comments by newsmen and broadcasters, the CBS program, apparently under Air Force guidance, if not control, may increase the number of citizens who reject the official explanations."

One of the assertions made on the CBS program was that none of our tracking cameras had ever photographed a UFO.

A former official of the Smithsonian Astrophysical Observatory wrote to NICAP: "During the time (twelve years) that I was with that organization the tracking cameras filmed a great many unidentified objects in conjunction with the routine filming of satellites. I would say that from twelve to fifteen percent of the pictures showed one or more unidentified objects. Due to the shortage of time, and the lack of official interest in them, there was no further study of the unidentified objects."

The *Christian Science Monitor* reported on May 3rd that the Smithsonian Astrophysical Observatory said that its "lower-powered tracking telescopes pick up hundreds of unidentified objects." Most of these they "regrettably" had no time to check out. In 1963, NICAP was given a few photographs taken by the Smithsonian Astrophysical Observatory Nunn-Baker cameras, showing trails of objects which did not coincide with those of known satellites. The source was A. B. Ledwith, former member of the satellite tracking program, who had carefully checked the reports against known objects.

Commenting on such assertions in a letter to *Science* magazine (October 21, 1966), Dr. J. Allen Hynek said that "UFO's have never been sighted on radar or photographed by meteor or satellite tracking cameras." This, Hynek wrote, "is not equivalent to saying that radar, meteor cameras, and satellite tracking stations have not picked up 'oddities' on their scopes or films, which have remained unidentified. It has been lightly assumed that although unidentified, the oddities were not unidentifiable as conventional objects.

"For these reasons I cannot dismiss the UFO phenomenon with a shrug. . . ."

In further refutation of the claims made on that CBS "documentary" of May 10th is the list of radar cases on page 76 of NICAP's *The UFO Evidence*. It is a list of specific cases, largely taken from USAF units or jet interceptor radar.

Following the Congressional hearing on April 5th NICAP Advisor William H. Hall, a veteran of many years in the field of electronics and radar, including both F-89 and F-94 systems, wrote to the Secretary of the Air Force. He challenged the Secretary's statement (to the Committee) that all radar cases involving UFOs had been explained. Mr. Hall appended a long list of radar sightings and asked for specific explanations for them. In its reply the Air Force disclaimed any knowledge or record of nearly half the cases on Hall's list, most of which were taken from Air Force Intelligence reports!

On May 4th, after he had returned to England from a

brief visit to the United States, Sir Bernard Lovell felt compelled to make a statement. The director of the Jodrell Bank radio astronomy station professed to be shocked by the amount of news space being given to the subject of UFOs in the United States.

"To my amazement," he told newsmen, "I found that the subject of flying saucers and unidentified flying objects is competing for space in newspapers almost with Viet Nam.

"It is an absurd situation that this fallacy, this form of escapism, should be in conflict with such realities as Viet Nam and real science.

"It is just escapism. It is all due to the fact that some people are not educated!"

(Ah, yes! Those "uneducated" astronomers, airline pilots, state and local police, and military and civilian radar operators!—F.E.)

Yet Sir Bernard's denunciation of UFOs as "escapism" was no more preposterous than a couple of other hypotheses offered as explanations during the year 1966.

There was, for instance, the theory advanced by Philip Klass, editor of the magazine *Aviation Week*, who contended that what he called a "corona discharge" from high voltage power lines might explain some of the reported sightings attributed to UFOs. He was referring to a phenomenon generally called "ball lightning." It was once dismissed by science as a figment of overexcited imaginations, but in the late 1940s and early 1950s it was given some test runs by the military, who hoped that it might develop into an anti-missile weapon.

According to Klass, corona discharge is most likely to occur when dust, salt deposits, or swarms of insects contaminate the power lines. It is also most likely to occur when there has been little rainfall to clean the lines. Klass noted in his magazine article that there had been a shortage of rainfall around Exeter, New Hampshire, prior to the reported UFO sightings there in 1965.

Mr. Klass's theory suffered from shortages other than water. The corona discharge theory had been checked out by the military and dismissed as meaningless, back in 1954. The small balls of light produced by induced corona discharge are much too small to represent an object the size of those reported by most observers—and only a fraction of a percent of the sightings occur on or near power lines.

The basic weakness of Mr. Klass's argument was that he was trying to explain a phenomenon with a theory.

I was on a television show with Mr. Klass in the summer of 1966, and he slyly held his blockbuster to the closing minutes of the program. Then he offered to pay me $10,000 if I could bring a living space creature to his office.

I explained to him that he was too late with too little —for there has been a standing offer of $50,000 for the same living space creature, an offer made in 1956 by a television station in Indianapolis (WTTV) and still standing, unclaimed.

Then I made him a counter offer: I would pay *him* $10,000 for any corona discharge he could produce outside a laboratory under conditions where it might be construed by the Air Force to be a UFO.

That ended *that* program.

Klass's Klassy Koronas had to share the spotlight in 1966 with the brain child of an amateur scientist in Denver, a fellow yclept, Norton T. Novitt. He earns his board and keep as a scientific illustrator for the U.S. Geologic Survey. But it was his hobby that got him into the papers in April of 1966.

161

Norton Novitt has noticed that over the last twenty years many UFOs have been seen glowing in the dark . . . and since his hobby was the electrical properties of insects—

Yep, that's just what old Norton figured out! Glowing insects—that's what some of them derned flying saucers were! Why he could even remember one time when he was on a Moonwatch Team back in the '50s. He was watching through a telescope one night when he saw a glowing spot moving too fast for a satellite, followed by another glowing dot. The two dots dived down and then stopped. To his amazement, he found that it was just a pair of lovestruck flying ants, landing on the door of a garage a few feet away.

Simple arithmetic indicates that the end result of a mating flight can be thirty-seven million insects. Now that's a heap of flying ants, shining or otherwise. What would they look like if they all glowed at once? Why, they would look like thirty-seven million glowing ants . . . and if they glowed in a disc-shaped formation they would look like a UFO.

Just one thing wrong with the theory, however. Ants do not usually glow . . . but Norton figured that they might if they picked up enough static electricity. Nobody knew; even the books couldn't tell him much. So he collected about two dozen flying ants and glued them on a pingpong ball. Then he attached the ball to a static generator and turned the crank. As the static electricity accumulated the ants began to glow. And as they say in the physics labs . . . "when you gotta glow, you gotta glow!"

But could the ants get enough of a charge to glow *without* the static generator?

Norton discovered that the ants had to have some moisture to enable them to glow . . . if they were thirsty they refused to perform. He theorized that if they went from one charged layer of air to another they might create enough of a potential difference to get them to go into corona (there's that word again!) if all the other conditions were favorable. Admittedly this is expecting a lot from a swarm of ants.

But there was an alternative. Some of Mr. Novitt's studies led him to believe that the ants would not have to change layers of air—they might be able to get a charge by rubbing against each other in flight—at least enough of a charge to glow for a fraction of a second.

One of those who was interested, so he said, in Novitt's glowing ants is Dr. Leonard Loeb, physics professor emeritus at the University of California. He said rather cautiously that Novitt's theories were "interesting . . . original . . . possibly right."

Dr. Loeb calculated that a fully charged swarm of thirty million flying ants would glow for not longer than one second, hardly long enough for the bewildered Air Force to send up their jets. Said Dr. Loeb, "There should be some provision in the theory for a greater duration of corona."

Swarms of insects on power lines can interfere with radio and television reception, the power companies have discovered, by causing static.

Still another form of static is generated by those who seek to explain UFOs as coronas, temperature inversions, or luminous flying ants.

"It's a flying object, but it's not exactly an unidentified flying object."

9

In retrospect, 1966 produced several important changes of direction in the field of the phenomenon known as Unidentified Flying Objects.

First was the "flap" which opened the year and continued almost unabated for several months thereafter, especially in the United States. It was one phase of this flap that provided so much cartoon material for the jokesmiths—the unforgettable "swamp gas" hypothesis, which plagues the Air Force and Dr. Hynek to this day. That was followed in a few days by the so-called "inquiry" conducted by the House Armed Services Committee, Congressman Mendel Rivers, chairman.

After these two definitive steps, there followed another rash of sightings, and in due time a surprisingly crisp and critical public statement by Dr. J. Allen Hynek. This in turn was followed by an interesting public statement by Dr. James McDonald, physicist of the University of Arizona, disclosing some material that he had found in the course of investigating the UFO records, and as the year went out in another flurry of sightings (including some photographs) Dr. Hynek made news again.

Please note that the hearing on the UFO problem was conducted by the Chairman of the powerful House Armed Services Committee. This is important. It is also significant. For it meant that the men in charge of the investigation were taking no chances that it might get out of hand; they conducted it themselves in order to be certain that no embarrassing questions were asked. There was no opportunity for a publicity-hungry chairman or member of a subcommittee to challenge the prepared statements offered by the witnesses from the Defense Department. Everything was cut and dried before that Committee. The Defense Department appeared, principally in the person of the Secretary of the Air Force, pleaded not guilty to the implied charge of concealing information about the ubiquitous UFOs. Then they paved the way for the selection of a civilian science group to "study" the problem and bowed out with a pat on the head from the Chairman of the Committee which had conducted the "hearing."

This technique is familiar to old hands in the nation's capital. I doubt that many, if any, of them were deceived for one minute by this maneuver. But I gather from reading the editorial comment around the nation that a good many editors failed to detect the hollow ring.

The hearing lasted exactly one day. This means that in one day the Committee went through the motions of investigating a complex problem of twenty years' standing! It served to create the impression that the matter had been looked into—and that the probers had found nothing. From reading the testimony I get the impression that they were being careful not to find anything.

So far, so good, from the standpoint of the censor group in the Pentagon. They had done their act before the Committee. They had read prepared statements. They had not been embarrassed by any pertinent or challenging questions. They had answered routine questions with routine replies.

No sweat.

It would be well for us to consider this development in the context of the contemporary circumstances.

It happened on April 5, 1966.

At that time the Air Force was on the defensive. Its public image was the worst in years, thanks to two monumental boo-boos—the "four stars" explanation of August 3, 1965, and the "swamp gas" proposal of March, 1966.

Together, these two blunders had brought a deluge of irate editorials. They had opened millions of eyes to the realization that the official explanations were less than candid—and ofttimes less than truthful. They had served to thrust the UFO matter right onto the front pages again. And they had stripped the Air Force of its credibility as a source of UFO information.

As they say in golf, they were in need of a good recovery shot. The proponents of the censorship policy in the Pentagon may have seen in the public clamor for a Congressional hearing the first step toward getting themselves, and the Air Force, off the hook and back into the good graces of the public and the press once more. Knowing that the public has a short memory, their first need was to stamp out the grass fire of irate public opinion, while they played for time, to let things simmer down.

The alleged hearing produced the headlines, studded with official denials of any deception.

So far—so good.

The same hearing also paved the way for a contract to be made with a group of civilian scientists—preferably connected with a major university—to conduct what is described as an unbiased evaluation of Air Force findings in UFO cases.

A contract was made with the University of Colorado.

The scientific study group is headed by a very eminent

man, Dr. Edward U. Condon, one-time head of the U.S. Bureau of Standards, a man renowned for his fine reputation and for his undeniable courage. In order to make this UFO study thorough and unbiased, Dr. Condon will need both those qualities.

If the scientific study by the University of Colorado does nothing else—even if it never submits a report—it will have been worth its weight in uranium to the censorship advocates in the Pentagon; for it will have diverted public attention from the beleaguered bunglers who brought the Air Force's prestige to a new low by their boners in 1965 and early 1966. In other words, the Pentagon cannot lose on this deal. At least they gain the time to refurbish the Air Force image; and if the final report of this committee of scientists should fail to be critical of the Air Force, then it will constitute a sort of daily-double for the Pentagon.

Some of the civilian UFO research groups have expressed the belief that the group at the University of Colorado will come up with a fresh, fine, definitive report—that it will ferret out the facts and falsehoods in the UFO phenomenon, and present the complete and correct picture to the public in its final report.

If the University of Colorado group can do that, then they have a right to regard themselves as miracle workers. If they can take $313,000 and conduct a lengthy and thorough investigation of such a protracted and complex problem, then they will have made the boys at Project Blue Book look like a bunch of clowns picking at their navels. Blue Book has spent millions of dollars over the better part of twenty years and has produced nothing definitive—at least for public consumption. How can anyone expect these civilian scientists to do better in less than two years, on a pinchpenny budget, what the Air Force has not been able to achieve in twenty?

According to the official announcement, Dr. Condon's group will be free to make its findings public, even if they should be contrary to Air Force views.

But isn't that a bit too much to expect?

The answer will be determined by the type of material the committee examines.

Shortly after the contract was signed, it was announced that the committee would be provided with "selected" material by the Air Force. This must have been a slip—for it was changed the following day to read that the committee would be provided with "material from the Air Force files." This again gets us to the same dilemma that put the House Armed Services Committee hearing in a strait-jacket—unless the scientists on the committee know which cases to request, they will get only the cases that someone wants them to get.

As of the first of March, 1967, the committee of scientists had shown no official interest in the pictures taken by two teenage brothers of Mt. Clemens, Michigan. (The pictures were said by Dr. J. Allen Hynek to be "free of any indication of a hoax"—and similar to other pictures the Air Force had shown to him in the course of his work as an Air Force consultant. That was a remarkable statement by a remarkable man—but for whatever reason the scientists at Colorado University took no interest in it—or the pictures.)

During the same time period they also gave the same treatment to two Polaroid pictures, taken of an object which hovered over a house in Zanesville, Ohio, on November 13, 1966. [These pictures bear a remarkable resemblance to the object photographed by Rex Heflin near Santa Ana, California, on August 3, 1965—also by Polaroid camera. See picture section.—F.E.] Months after the Zanesville pictures were published, the scientific probers had shown no interest in them.

If the committee depends on the Air Force to furnish it with "selected" cases it would be ridiculous to expect the Air Force to provide any material that could end up by exposing the falsity of the Blue Book claims. Those "selected" cases would almost certainly be selected to enable the committee to arrive at a predetermined result— the tacit endorsement of the policy of censorship by the final announcement by the committee that it had been unable to find anything that disagreed with the publicized claims.

I wish to re-emphasize that here, as in the so-called "hearing" before the House Armed Services Committee, the end result will depend largely on the material that is examined. The "hearing" asked the customary questions and received the usual replies. Consequently, and predictably, it found nothing.

If the committee of scientists at Colorado University is required—or willing—to depend on handouts from the military—for whatever reason—then it cannot be fully efficient or objective in its assigned task.

Unless the committee can study the pictures and compare them, unless it can question and interview the airline pilots and the military pilots who have seen these objects, and unless it can talk to the numerous professional astronomers who have reported the UFOs—then it cannot have a good foundation on which to predicate its conclusions. This is precisely the kind of evidence on which the military bases its statements—and it is the evidence on which the committee must make its findings, whatever they may be.

If the Condon committee, hampered by shortage of manpower and shortage of funds, finds itself unable to do a thorough job of seeking out and examining the evidence, such as it is, then it is conceivable that it might end up by presenting a statement hinting that the UFOs are nonexistent.

The real danger here is that such a statement would be accepted at face value by many persons who were not aware that it was based on inadequate investigation.

The manner in which the decision to turn the problem over to a civilian group was arrived at; the revealing statement that the committee would be given "selected" material (hastily corrected); the big assignment and the small budget; and above all the desperate Air Force need for time, to restore their public image—all these factors lead me to believe that (barring a miracle) the report may shed little light on the UFO phenomenon, but much light on an adroit public relations maneuver which bailed out the censorship proponents in the Pentagon.

I sincerely hope that my fears prove groundless, and there is at least one bit of information which may be a straw in the wind.

A member of the Condon Committee, project co-ordinator Robert Low, personally re-visited the scene on the highway near Santa Ana, California, with Rex Heflin, who snapped three pictures of an alleged UFO there on August 3, 1965.

Heflin's pictures were branded a hoax by Project Blue Book director Major Hector Quintanilla. But examination of the official staff report does not substantiate Quintanilla's claims: The staff report merely disagrees with Heflin's estimate of the size and probable altitude.

After visiting the scene of the incident with Heflin (a Los Angeles County highway official) and after questioning him at length, Professor Low told newsmen that the Condon committee had concluded that Heflin's pictures were among the ". . . top four or five examples of photographic evidence of the existence of UFOs.

"Nothing has happened to change that appraisal of their status as among the very best flying saucer photos anywhere."

For eighteen years Dr. J. Allen Hynek has been the chief scientific advisor to the Air Force on the problem of UFOs. As such, he has been privy to much of the material the Air Force has garnered over those years. And he was, and presumably is, under security regulations which would prevent him from discussing publicly much of what he has seen and heard in his official capacity.

(When I was offered a job in this general area in mid-1954, I refused after I learned that I would be muzzled by security. The military officials who made the offer could only assure me that it dealt with a very important topic in which I had shown a great deal of interest. Girls? They shook their heads. Flying saucers? They did not reply. —F.E.)

After eighteen years in his high-level capacity with the official UFO investigations, what motivated Dr. Hynek to speak out so abruptly and so bluntly, I do not know. There was no indication that he and the Air Force had any differences, either in policy or pronouncements, prior to March of 1966. But then—Ah! Methinks we have a clue!

That was when Dr. Hynek was called in by the harassed Air Force to explain the sightings around the University of Michigan. And as we have seen, he "suggested" that the answer might be swamp gas—which, he discovered, can be explosive when offered to newsmen in a closed room.

The dear old Doc became the butt of jokes based on the "swamp gas" line. At first he was startled, then he was amused, and finally he became annoyed.

Writing in the *Saturday Evening Post* for December 17, 1966, Dr. Hynek explained the background for his gaseous remark.

Acting on orders from the Air Force to investigate the reported sightings around the University of Michigan, he says that when he got to Michigan he found the situation so charged with emotion that it was impossible for him to conduct any serious investigation. The Air Force left him, he writes, almost completely on his own. Continuing, and I quote Dr. Hynek: ". . . sometimes I had to fight my way through clusters of reporters who were surrounding the key witnesses whom I had to interview."

Then, says Dr. Hynek, "The entire region was gripped with near-hysteria."

[That is quite understandable—possibly a side-effect of swamp gas.—F.E.]

Dr. Hynek continues:

"In the midst of this confusion, I got a message from the Air Force: There would be a press conference, and I would issue a statement about the cause of the sightings. It did me no good to protest, to say that as yet I had no real idea what had caused the reported sightings in the swamps. I was to have a press conference, ready or not."

The Doctor says that he remembered a phone call from a botanist calling to his attention the phenomenon of swamp gas, caused by decaying vegetable matter. He says that this was mentioned in his handout at the press conference as a "possible" answer—and the cat was out of the bag.

There is an interesting sidelight here which I have very good reason to believe is true—for the man who reported it to me is a network newsman whom I have known and worked with for years . . . and who was present at the time.

According to my informant, he overheard an argument between Dr. Hynek and the Air Force men, in a room not far from where the press was waiting for the answer. He says that the words between the Doctor and the military were heated . . . he got the impression that Dr. Hynek was objecting to being rushed into a press conference when he was not prepared . . . and that he was especially resentful at being told to include the swamp gas bit.

The name of Major Hector Quintanilla, head of Project Blue Book, kept cropping up in the argument, and my friend received the impression that Dr. Hynek was being told that Major Quintanilla was ordering him to make the statement.

If this interpretation is correct, it may help to explain some later developments, as we shall see.

The upshot of the swamp gas explanation was that Dr. Hynek, as the individual who offered the suggestion, was tarred with the brush—and the Air Force, as part and parcel of the "investigation" which produced this farcical climax, was the target for another barrage of editorials and cartoons.

Official statements on UFOs had reached a new low.

* * * * *

Like a bolt from the blue was Dr. Hynek's letter to *Science* magazine, listing several "public misconceptions" regarding the UFO problems. Although Dr. Hynek does not say so, the alleged misconceptions are actually the result of false statements by Project Blue Book. And Dr. Hynek released his letter to the press on August 27th, after *Science* magazine "did not see fit" to publish it.

Hynek made it clear that in being critical of the conduct of the official UFO investigations he was not being critical of the Air Force. Instead, he asserted, he was speaking out in his personal capacity of a scientist who was increasingly concerned about the UFO problem. (He called it "one of the great mysteries of the twentieth century" and noted that in spite of a "great volume" of substantial UFO data, it is being ignored by scientists.)

The scientific consultant to the Air Force on UFOs called attention to the similarity between scientific treatment of the UFOs and the manner in which science had steadfastly denied the existence of meteorites—on the self-evident fact that since there were no stones in the sky, it was ridiculous to believe that stones could fall from the sky. [Dr. Hynek might have included the scornful scientific attitude toward the duck-billed platypus of Australia when it was first discovered. Many scientists refused to examine the creature, contending that it was contrary to nature, therefore it had to be a fraud. And he might have called attention to the editorial attitude of the *Scientific American,* which, in January of 1906, more than two years after the *Wright* brothers' flights at Kitty Hawk, ran an editorial ridiculing the idea that men could fly in heavier-than-air machines!—F.E.]

In his letter of August, 1966, which was first rejected by *Science* magazine, Dr. Hynek makes seven points. He calls these misconceptions about the UFO phenomenon, without mentioning the Project Blue Book statements from which they were taken.

1. *That only UFO "buffs" (enthusiasts) report UFO's.*
Hynek says: "The exact opposite is much nearer the truth. Only a negligible handful of reports submitted to the Air Force, or to any other organization as far as I know, are from the 'true believers' who attend UFO conventions and who are members of the 'gee whiz' groups."

The truly puzzling reports, he adds, come from people who have not given much, if any, thought to UFOs, and who generally "consider such reports from others to be bunk, until they are shaken by their own experience."

2. *UFOs are reported by unreliable, unstable, and uneducated people.*
"While that is true of some reports," says Hynek, "even greater numbers are reported by reliable, stable and educated people. Dullards rarely overcome the inertia and get down to writing a report."

3. *UFOs are never reported by scientifically trained people.*
"This is unequivocally false," says Dr. Hynek, who adds: "Some of the very best, most coherent reports, come from scientifically trained people." He notes that such people are often reluctant to make a report for fear of being publicly identified with the subject.

(Examples of such cases in support of Dr. Hynek's contention would include the two UFOs seen and reported by famed astronomer H. Percy Wilkins in 1952; by astronomer Seymour Hess, May 20, 1950; and by an Apollo Space Project engineer, Julian Sandoval, near Coralles, New Mexico, on June 23, 1966, at 3:42 a.m. In addition to being in charge of the Apollo Project electrical power and environmental control, Mr. Sandoval is a former Air Force pilot and navigator with seven thousand hours of flying time.

In a signed report to NICAP, published in the *NICAP Investigator*, Sandoval reports seeing the object while he was driving on Highway 85, near Coralles, when he spotted the thing hanging at an estimated altitude of about twelve thousand feet above the antenna tower at Sandia Crest, Albuquerque. The main body of the thing was tetrahedron in shape and emitted a bright incandescent glow similar to that of an ordinary electric light bulb. At the tail, he reported, there were four blue-green lights.

"It was totally unlike anything we have!" he told NICAP.

Mr. Sandoval reported that he watched the object for fifty-one minutes, part of the time through binoculars. He estimated that the craft was three hundred feet long and says that it was clearly visible in the moonlight. The aerospace engineer noted that when the thing changed position it brightened considerably, leading him to the conclusion that the luminescence was linked with the propulsion system.

In a separate statement to NICAP, Sandoval stated that he was able to estimate the length of the craft by using the Sandia antenna tower as a reference point when the object was directly above it. The UFO traveled approximately twenty-two miles at an average speed of thirty-five miles per hour, his report continues. During this time it slowly descended to about nine thousand feet altitude. Following

179

this maneuver, it went into a vertical climb at fantastic speed.

"Its final speed was about Mach 6 [six times the speed of sound] or better," Sandoval writes.—F.E.)

Other competent witnesses include astronauts James McDivitt, Michael Collins, and John W. Young. McDivitt photographed an egg-shaped object with a visible contrail as it circled his capsule over the Pacific in June of 1955 (see picture section). NICAP member Zan Overall wrote to NASA's Manned Spacecraft Center regarding the UFO being described by astronauts Collins and Young during their Gemini mission in July, 1966. Overall received a reply from Howard Gibbons, Chief, News Service Branch, Public Affairs Office. The letter notes that Collins and Young had previously sighted two objects (later "identified" as fragments of a rocket) and then adds: "Astronaut Collins reported a second sighting of a space object, probably in the vicinity of Australia, later in the Gemini 10 mission. It was moving north to south against a star field in an (apparent) polar orbit. Identity of the object was not determined."

Dr. Hynek's statement that competent and credible witnesses *do* see and report UFOs is fully attested.

4. *That UFOs are never seen at close range or seen clearly, but are always vaguely reported and seen under conditions of great uncertainty.*

Dr. Hynek says that when he speaks of "puzzling reports" he excludes all reports which could be covered by the above description. He adds, "I have in my files several hundred reports which are real brain teasers and could easily be made the subject of profitable discussion among physical and social scientists alike."

5. *The Air Force has no evidence that UFOs are extra-terrestrial or represent advanced technology of any kind.*

"The unidentified cases remain unidentified and hence cannot be used in answering this question. As long as there are 'unidentifieds' the question must obviously remain open. If we knew what they were they would no longer be UFO. . . ."

In support of the extraterrestrial hypothesis is the fact that the chunk of iron shot off one of the discs near Washington, D.C., in 1952 was found, upon analysis, to possess some peculiar characteristics. (See *Flying Saucers—Serious Business*, "Pick up the Pieces" for details.) Further evidence of the advanced technology involved is to be found in the UFOs' ability to accelerate at a rate far beyond anything man has developed and in their well-known ability to travel at very high speed without producing a sonic boom. In August of 1965, the Air Force radar base on the Keweenaw Peninsula reported that it had tracked several UFOs across Lake Superior at speeds around ninety-six hundred miles per hour . . . but minus the sonic boom.

6. *UFO reports are generated by publicity.*

Dr. Hynek agrees that this factor is at work when sightings are widely publicized—that persons are thus encouraged to report sightings who might otherwise not do so.

"On the other hand," he says, "some of the sightings that are reported at times of high publicity come from persons of reliability who request anonymity, and who state that if they had not heard of reports from other ostensibly reliable persons they would never have mentioned their own experiences for fear of ridicule."

I can attest to this type of witness from personal experience. In the summer of 1965 I was making a speech in a large midwestern city. At the conclusion of the talk I was approached by a man who asked me if I had time to come across the street for a brief talk with the president of a bank. I went—and the bank president and his wife told me of a frightening experience they had undergone about three months before . . . in March of 1965 . . . as they drove across New Mexico.

They said that they preferred to drive after midnight, when the roads were relatively free of traffic. On this night the wife was driving. They were about twenty miles west of Santa Rosa and it was about 1 a.m. Suddenly a bright greenish light appeared in the sky ahead of them. It was closing rapidly. Their car was alone on that stretch of highway. The lady pulled off alongside the road to observe the phenomenon better. They estimate that they sat there for not more than a minute and by that time the light was so close—and so brilliant—that it was blinding. The object had stopped about a hundred yards down the highway, and about twenty feet above the surface.

The banker and his wife both admitted that they were badly frightened by this time. They locked the car doors and bent over below the dash, to get out of that beam of light. After a couple of minutes of this the light switched off and the highway was clear. They waited for a moment or two to regain their composure and then pulled back onto the road.

By the time they had gone not more than half a mile they discovered that they were being paced by the object again . . . this time it was moving along abreast of their car over the fields an estimated two hundred yards to their right. A brilliant white beam of light shot down underneath the object at intervals which they estimated to be of about five seconds. Once the greenish beam played on their car for a couple of seconds. Then both the greenish and the white light went out and the object was evidently gone, disappearing as swiftly and as mysteriously as it had appeared. The banker and his wife were both badly shaken by their experience. They said they had not told anyone about it before telling me, for fear of being regarded as a bit nutty.

A somewhat similar case involved a prominent member of the West Virginia Women's Club, a former officer of the club. I was speaking to their convention in Huntington, several years ago and, when I asked if anyone present had ever seen one of these UFOs, much to everybody's surprise this lady stood up. She said that she and her husband, a well-known surgeon in West Virginia, had had an experience about a year before as they visited a farm they owned in Ohio. They had not discussed it with anyone, she told us, for fear of being ridiculed, but that morning they had decided that it was time to tell someone—so she told the assemblage.

She and her husband had driven to their isolated Ohio farm on a wintry Sunday afternoon. They were returning to the highway just about sundown. Suddenly she noticed a shiny thing rising slowly from behind some willows along a creek bed. She called it to the attention of her husband and the doctor stopped the car in order to see better. By this time the thing was above the willows. It looked shiny and metallic. It was circular, perhaps twenty-five or thirty feet in diameter, flat on the bottom with a narrow rim and a low dome on top, possibly five feet thick. They heard no sound and saw no visible means of propulsion. As they sat in their car, the strange object moved slowly and deliberately toward them. The doctor hastily locked the doors. Both he and his wife were terrified, she told us. They were unable to drive—virtually unable to move— while that disc hovered over the car for a minute or so— then moved about fifty feet ahead of the car and hovered over the road for another minute. Then it began to gain both speed and altitude and was soon out of their sight. They had told only the editor of their local paper, a personal friend, with the understanding that he would not publish the story, but they did want to be on record.

Dr. Hynek doubtless has many such cases in his files and his statement hinting at that is readily acceptable to me.

7. UFOs have never been sighted on radar or photographed by meteor- or satellite-tracking cameras.

In evaluating Hynek's reply to that oft-quoted canard, it should be kept in mind that not only did he have access to the Air Force records of such cases but he also served as Associate Director of the Smithsonian Astrophysical Observatory from 1956 to 1960, where he was also chief of upper atmosphere studies and satellite tracking.

Radar, meteor and satellite-tracking gear have all picked up oddities that could not be identified, says Dr. Hynek. "One should consider such things as the odd photograph of a 'retrograde satellite' taken in 1958, and the puzzling reports from several Moonwatch teams during the International Geophysical Year project."

By "retrograde satellite" he means an object circling Earth from east to west, *which no manmade object does.*

In addition, Hynek says that he has seen photographs taken by satellite-tracking cameras which contained unexplained streaks which he admitted were never identified.

Why did Dr. J. Allen Hynek write for publication such a letter, challenging the seven claims which had been made so frequently by the staff at Project Blue Book?

The Doctor says that he wanted to call to the attention of his colleagues in various fields of science the fact that here was a phenomenon which was worthy of their serious consideration, for, he writes, "I have seen a pattern emerging from my many years of monitoring the phenomenon."

This pattern, he explains, involves a class of motions, such as wobbling and hovering and rapid take-offs. It also includes geometric configurations, disc and oval and cigar shapes. And there seemed to be a consistent pattern of luminescent characteristics, including flashing lights and brilliant beams of light from the objects.

"This pattern suggests that something is going on," Dr. Hynek says. "Good physical explanations may exist—indeed, must exist in a rational world—and this is why I am calling this to the attention of science."

Dr. Hynek's letter, which *Science* magazine first refused to publish, later appeared in that publication with the explanation that they had first rejected it because they had carried an article on flying saucers in a recent issue. It was possibly better than no explanation at all.

While Dr. Hynek was trying to bring this subject to the attention of his myopic colleagues, the UFOs themselves were doing their bit around the globe, as we shall see.

On August 7th, the ultra-conservative *Washington* (D.C.) *Evening Star* ran a full-page article FLYING SAUCERS AGAIN: DO YOU BELIEVE IN THEM? It was written by a former editor of the Air Force *Air Intelligence Digest*, Lieutenant Colonel Charles Cooke, USAF Retired, and it stressed the writer's belief that the UFOs were not only real, but that they were of extraterrestrial origin. He declared that he first arrived at this conclusion in 1948 and is today what he calls an "implacable" believer in UFOs.

The *Evening Star* identifies Lieutenant Colonel Cooke as the founder of the *Air Intelligence Digest* and later editor of the Far East Air Force's *FEAF Intelligence Roundup,* published in Tokyo. He identifies himself as the man who suggested the name "Project Blue Book" for the investigative body of that title. He received several citations for the caliber of his work with the Air Force, including one for his editorship of the *Intelligence Digest,* from General Charles Cabell, Director of Intelligence for the Air Force at that time, and another for editing the Far East Intelligence publication in Tokyo from General Donald R. Zimmerman.

The article says:

"From 1948 to 1952 at the Pentagon and from 1952 to 1955 in Tokyo, my desk was one of several across which flowed 'information copies' of the steadily increasing stream of UFO sightings being reported to the Air Force."

Continuing, he says:

"Despite the fact that I had no UFO responsibilities, no one in the USAF assembly line down which the reports passed read and pondered them more absorbedly, more dedicatedly, than I.

"I was especially interested in three aspects. . . .

"One: I duly noted the myriad 'explanations' given out by the Blue Book staff—of sightings which they evaluated as mistakenly identified stars, planets, comets, meteors, ionized clouds, airplanes, helicopters, balloons, auroral streamers, birds, reflected lights, mirages, marsh gas

186

—or as illusions, delusions, hallucinations, psychic aberrations, hoaxes, publicity stunts, gags, pranks, etc.

"Two: I noted that the hard core of 'unexplained' cases fluctuated from as high as 7% to as low as 2%—but significantly never lower.

"Third: I noticed that the date of the first UFO sighting was generally given—and still is—as June 24, 1947."

Colonel Cooke points out that that was merely the date when the UFO were first seen in numbers over the northwestern part of the United States. (They had been seen in numbers over northwestern Russia and the Scandinavian countries in 1946—just one year after man exploded his first atomic devices—which may be pure coincidence, of course.)

Continuing, Cook writes: "My lifelong hobby of astronomy, together with what I regard as overwhelming affirmative evidence, incline me toward the belief that UFOs are 'real' and of celestial origin—interplanetary or interstellar."

In conclusion, he offered this declaration from Joseph Bryan III, Colonel USAF, Retired, former special assistant to the Secretary of the Air Force (1952-1953) and former staff member to General Lauris Norstad, then Supreme Allied Commander of NATO. Quoting Colonel Bryan from NICAP, of which Bryan is a member of the Board of Governors:

"It is my opinion that the UFOs reported by competent observers are devices under intelligent control; that their speeds, maneuvers, and other technical evidence prove them superior to any aircraft or space devices now produced on earth; and that these UFOs are interplanetary devices systematically observing the earth, either manned or under remote control, or both."

187

Finding such an article in the *Washington Evening Star* was a profound shock to me, although it was a pleasant surprise.

I must admit that I would hardly have been more astonished had I met Brigham Young, arm in arm with Lydia E. Pinkham.

(The splendid public reception given to Lieutenant Colonel Cooke's article probably was instrumental in paving the way for the *Star*'s serialization of my book, *Flying Saucers—Serious Business*, a few months later.)

If Dr. Hynek's letter was disturbing to the boys at Project Blue Book, they had another shock coming.

On October 10th, they got the other barrel.

The gunner on that date was Dr. James E. McDonald and he was speaking to the District of Columbia chapter of the American Meteorological Society. Dr. McDonald is Senior Physicist, Institute of Atmospheric Physics, and Professor, Department of Meteorology, at the University of Arizona, Tucson. He is also a member of the National Academy of Sciences Committee on Weather and Climate Modification; he served four years in Naval Intelligence in World War II and is a former research physicist at the University of Chicago.

Dr. McDonald, as Dr. Hynek had done before him, spoke critically of the manner in which the Air Force had conducted its "investigations" of UFO sightings cases. He condemned the widely publicized Project Blue Book statistical reports as *"utterly worthless."* (This echoes the conclusions of the *Yale Scientific Magazine,* Yale University, April, 1963.)

"The work of independent organizations such as the National Investigations Committee on Aerial Phenomena [NICAP] impress me as being more thorough and open-

188

minded than those of Project Blue Book," said Dr. McDonald. "Their efforts should be exploited and incorporated into all future studies."

(NICAP was invited to participate in the program of the Condon committee at the University of Colorado about a month after Dr. McDonald's speech.)

In the spring of 1966, the physicist obtained a small grant from the University of Arizona to probe the UFO phenomenon more thoroughly. He visited NICAP headquarters in Washington and examined their voluminous files. Then he went to Wright-Patterson Air Force Base at Dayton to inspect their files and to interview Major Quintanilla. It was there that Dr. McDonald found written evidence of a high-level program to have the Air Force "play down" UFO reports.

"A part of the background of the manner in which Blue Book has handled the UFO problem in the past dozen years is to be found in the complete report of the 1953 Robertson Panel." (That scientific board, headed by H. P. Robertson of the California Institute of Technology, took the position that the American public is "gullible" and "incompetent observers."—F.E.)

Of the Robertson Panel, Dr. McDonald said:

"That scientific panel [also] concluded that there was no strong evidence of any hostile UFO action. The Central Intelligence Agency, represented at the policy-drafting sessions closing the activities of the Robertson Panel, requested that the Air Force adopt a policy of systematic 'debunking of flying saucer reports' in order to decrease public attention to UFOs. The reasons for this were associated with the 1952 wave of UFO reports, the largest wave ever recorded in the United States [prior to 1965.—F.E.]. The 1952 wave was possibly exceeded in intensity by the

1954 wave of sightings in France. So many UFO reports were flooding the air bases of this country in 1952 that the CIA regarded them as creating a national security problem: In the event of an enemy attack on this country, the clogging of military intelligence channels with large numbers of reports of the evidently non-hostile UFOs was regarded as an unacceptable hazard."

(The UFO visits to Washington, D.C., in July-August of 1952 confronted the authorities with a serious problem: They either had to admit that unknown craft of unknown origin and purpose were visiting the nation's capital and that they could not prevent it—or they had to *pretend* that the UFOs were nonexistent, while they tried to find some way to cope with them. That was the course they chose— the course of deception and censorship. The official order establishing the ground rules and the penalties for violation of the censorship is known as JANAP 146. It covers all the military agencies of the U.S. government.—F.E.)

"This CIA request, made in January of 1953," Dr. Mc-Donald told the Meteorological Society, "was followed by the promulgation in August, 1953, of the Air Force Regulation 200-2, which produced a sharp drop-off in public reporting of UFO sights by forbidding the release, at Air Base level, of any information on sightings of unidentified aerial phenomena. All sighting reports were to be funneled through Project Blue Book, where they have been largely categorized as conventional objects, with—in my opinion— very little attention to scientific considerations. The strictures implicit in AFR 200-2 were made even more severe in the promulgation of JANAP 146, which made any public release of UFO information at Air Base level (by any of the military services and, under certain conditions, commercial airlines) a crime punishable with fines up to $10,000 and imprisonment up to ten years.

"These regulations have not only cut off almost all useful reports from military pilots, tower operators and ground crews, but even more serious from a scientific standpoint has been their drastic effect on non-availability of UFO radar sightings where disclosed; since then, military radar sightings have been scientifically compromised by confusing details and by allusions to 'weather inversions' or 'electronic malfunctions' whenever word of radar observations accidentally leaked out in the midst of a UFO episode. Air Force Regulation 200-2 contained the specific admonishment that 'Air Force activities must reduce the percentage of unidentifieds to the minimum.'

"This has been achieved."

Noting that thousands of credible and competent witnesses had reported these objects during the past twenty years alone, Dr. McDonald said that his conclusions were drawn from a careful, intensive study of the UFO problem. Atmospheric phenomena, such as ball lightning, mirages, scintillation, parhelia, anomalous radar propagation, etc., have been invoked to account for many UFO reports, and such explanations have been seriously misapplied. The physicist cited examples to demonstrate how the explanations failed to fit the facts.

Citing these numerous and important discrepancies, Dr. McDonald called for serious and intensive scientific scrutiny and study of the problem, which, as the military admits, is not a military problem, since by their own statements the UFOs present no threat to the nation.

In conclusion, Dr. McDonald said to his fellow scientists:

191

"It is important to stress that there are baffling aspects of the available, credibly reported, UFO cases. It is not possible to offer any pat explanations of the temporal and spatial distribution of the sightings. I reject as ill-considered any demands that one may now be able to explain why the UFOs, if extra-terrestrial, so often appear in relatively remote areas; why nighttime observations are more common than daytime; why we have no substantial evidence of any 'contact' or 'communication,' etc.

"Intriguing as those questions may be, they immediately plunge one into completely unsupported speculations. The present urgent need is for much more scientific examination of the available UFO evidence in order to establish, or to reject, as the case may be, the very interesting possibility that these aerial objects may be some type of extra-terrestrial probes.

"The extra-terrestrial theory is the least unsatisfactory hypothesis to explain the phenomenon of the UFOs."

"How long do you suppose they'll go on shutting their eyes to the obvious?"

10

The most frequent question concerning the UFOs is—"Where do they come from?"

The answer is—"Nobody knows." It is possible that they may have more than one point of origin. Manmade space probes already have two sources right here on this tiny planet. The craft we are sending out into the solar system have similar goals but are different in both shape and size. The same may hold true of the Unidentified Flying Objects—different craft (and perhaps different types of operators) from different origins. But as of now, no man can do more than speculate as to where they originate.

2. *"Is it true that UFOs are not tracked on radar?"*

It is not true. Thousands of maneuvering UFOs have been tracked on radars, both civil and military. The most famous trackings were those around Washington, D.C., in the summer of 1952. The Civil Aeronautics Administration published a restricted booklet showing how the things performed on radar on the night of August 13, 1952. In August of 1965 the Air Force Radar Base on the Keweenaw Peninsula reported watching a flight of UFOs on radar over Lake Superior. In May of 1964 the officials at Holloman Air Force Base, which guards White Sands Missile Range in New Mexico, reported that their radar had been tracking a UFO for two days, at intervals. Do not be misled by statements, *whatever the source,* which assert or imply that UFOs are not tracked on radar.

3. *"Why don't we ever get any pieces of UFOs?"*

The head of the Canadian UFO program (comparable in purpose to our Blue Book program) said in an interview, which was tape recorded with his permission, that the U.S. Air Force lent to the Canadian UFO project a fragment of a "flying saucer" for examination. Wilbert Smith, head of the Canadian project, described the sample as having been shot off the rim of a small UFO during the big flap of 1952 near Washington. He said that metallurgists had determined that it was pure iron, differing from conventionally worked iron only in the globular structure of which it was composed. He also said that he had to return the unused portion of the specimen to an agency higher in government than the Air Force, but he declined to identify the agency.

There are other officially identified fragment cases: The molten tin that dribbled from a malfunctioning UFO over Campinas, Brazil, on December 14, 1954. The empty outer shell of a UFO recovered from the island of Spitzbergen and reported by the Norwegian government in the summer of 1952.

There are probably other specimens of extraterrestrial hardware, but the three I have just itemized are ample to refute the assertion that none exists.

4. *"Has anyone ever actually talked to the operators of these craft, or ridden in a UFO?"*

The only flights human beings have ever made in UFOs appear to be flights of fancy. (See Chapter Seven.)

5. *"Who was the first astronaut to see a UFO in orbit?"*

On the record it was Major Gordon Cooper, over Muchea Tracking Station near Perth, Australia, on his final orbit of Earth on a night in May of 1963. The object which approached him was also seen by the two hundred persons at the tracking station. It was reported twice on the NBC radio network before Cooper had been picked up by the rescue craft. He was not permitted to comment on it.

There was one other astronaut who reportedly saw a UFO at close range while he was in orbit. Scientists who are connected with the space work tell me that because of the emotional shock he experienced he was not permitted to go aloft again, although he eventually recovered from the effects of the incident and is apparently normal and healthy at the present time (1967).

Astronaut Major James McDivitt made a picture of a glowing egg-shaped object which approached the capsule in which he was orbiting with Major Edward White in 1965. (See photographs of both sides of this object in picture section.)

6. *"Do UFOs show any interest in our experimental high-altitude planes?"*

In April of 1962, Major Joe Walker was test-flying the X-15 rocket plane at better than two thousand miles per hour when his rear-facing cameras filmed five disc-shaped objects flying in echelon formation behind his plane. (They were later explained as "ice-flakes"—presumably the prelude to "swamp gas.")

On July 29, 1966, the Defense Department revealed that one of the high-altitude U-2 planes which make regular flights over Cuba was missing. Significantly perhaps, the

197

official statement said that the pilot, Captain Robert D. Hickman, could not be contacted during the flight. There may have been a good reason for that.

Captain Hickman had taken off from Barksdale Air Force Base in Louisiana on the morning of July 28th on a routine mission. That routine mission took the plane southward across the tip of Florida. On that course he was headed across Cuba at extremely high altitude. The Pentagon said pointedly that there was "positively no indication of surface-to-air missile activity from Cuba." Please note that statement.

The first indication that something was amiss came when the radar in Florida noticed that the U-2 did not change course as anticipated after it crossed Florida. Radio messages sent to the high-flying spy plane went unacknowledged. The U-2 droned serenely on across the Caribbean somewhere above seventy thousand feet, seemingly oblivious to the frantic attempts to communicate being made by several bases, especially Albrook Air Force Base in Panama.

The official statement established that the Pentagon position was that Pilot Hickman had lost consciousness due to a malfunction of his oxygen equipment, which at that altitude would have had lethal consequences in seconds.

But there is another angle of this case which is noteworthy, perhaps more so than we realize.

As Captain Hickman flew over the Caribbean, later to crash in Bolivia, the radar at Air Rescue Center in the Canal Zone admittedly made an interesting discovery . . . Captain Hickman had company up there. An Unidentified Object of some sort approached his flight path—and the Base was unable to reach Hickman by radio. The presence of the UFO was announced by the Associated Press;

198

then that aspect of the story was promptly squelched, although it originated in a statement from Southern Command Headquarters.

Had someone talked out of turn? It would appear so.

This would seem to be an excellent answer to the question of whether UFOs approach our high-altitude planes.

By official admission it could not have been a missile.

By official admission it was a UFO which approached the doomed plane. Whether it contributed to the fatal crash which ensued is problematical, and I think improbable.

But it did indicate an interest in one of our high-altitude planes, and that fact was officially confirmed, even though the confirmation was brief.

7. *"What were the strange metal spheres which were found—or reportedly found—in the Australian desert a few years ago?"*

They *were* found. It is a strange story with a unique sequel.

On April 8, 1963, an Australian ranger named J. McClure brought in from the desert of New South Wales a shiny metal sphere about fourteen inches in diameter, weighing twelve pounds. It had been spotted from overhead by a plane which was crossing a part of the desert that had been shunned by human beings for at least fifty years. McClure turned his find over to the government for further investigation.

On June 28th, at a point about sixty miles from the scene of McClure's discovery, another shiny metal sphere was found. Like its predecessor, it was perfectly smooth, brightly polished, and without any aperture of any kind to give access to the interior. It was about sixteen inches in diameter and weighed slightly more than eighteen pounds.

The third of these unusual spheres was picked up on July 12th, near Muloorina, New South Wales. It was about six inches in diameter, weighed seven pounds, and had one small aperture, about half an inch in diameter, which enabled investigators to ascertain that the sphere was lined with lead.

Mr. Allen Fairhall, the Australian Minister of Supply, went before the House of Representatives on April 30, 1963, to brief them on the matter. He said that Australian scientists were puzzled by the objects. He added that they had no idea what they were or where they came from. And he also stated that efforts to open the first sphere with drills and hacksaws had been futile.

In late 1964 I wrote to the Australian Embassy in Washington, D.C., to inquire what the final determination in this peculiar case had been.

Two months later I received a reply. It came not from the Embassy in Washington but from the Australian Consulate in New York City! And it assured me that the metal spheres had been only three freezing units from an old type of electric refrigerator!

If that was an "explanation" it leaves much unexplained.

For instance, what caliber of scientists would not have recognized a common freezing unit from a refrigerator?

And if it was such a prosaic device, how did the two large spheres function, since there were no apertures through which the fluid or gas could have circulated?

8. *"How many countries have reported UFO sightings?"*
Since the UFOs first appeared in numbers in 1946, they have been reported by every nation on Earth. But in re-

cent years most of the reports seem to be concentrated over the more industrialized nations.

9. *"Have any professional astronomers reported seeing UFOs?"*

Many of them have described watching the strange objects called UFOs. Dr. Seymour Hess; Frank Halstead, for twenty-five years head of Darling Observatory; Dr. H. Percy Wilkins, former head of the British Selenological Society; and Nobel Prize winner Bart Bok, of Mt. Stromlo Observatory in Australia—to name only a few of them.

10. *"Why don't professional astronomers ever report that they have seen a UFO through their big telescopes?"*

For one thing, the telescopes are made for viewing at tremendous distances. Their field of view is extremely small. The difficulty of seeing relatively small objects at close range with observatory equipment is borne out by the results of a questionnaire which I sent to one hundred professional astronomers in 1964. I asked them how many commercial airliners they had seen in flight with their telescopes. Not much to my surprise none of them had ever seen a single airliner in those circumstances. This does not prove that airliners do not exist; instead, it points up the difficulties of seeing small moving objects at close range with gear that is not designed for that purpose.

11. *"Are any of these UFOs manned?"*

If by manned we mean operated by human beings of earthly origin, the answer is negative. But if we extend the term "manned" to include living operators of unknown origin, the answer seems to be "yes." In fact, the *Air Force In-*

201

telligence Manual (AFM-200-3) of September, 1953, is illustrated with a drawing of a new-type UFO which was phasing out the original "flying-saucer" disc at that time. And this new double-convex UFO in the Air Force drawing had a transparent dome for the unmistakable use of one or more living operators.

The most credible descriptions of these operators are remarkably uniform, regardless of what part of Earth the reports come from: small humanoid types of creatures, wearing shiny coverall type suits and generally wearing transparent helmets. (Do you suppose they are trying to give up smoking?)

12. *"Is there government censorship of UFO information?"*

There has been regulated censorship of UFO information since 1952, when the order known as JANAP 146 went into effect as a result of the furor over the sightings in and around the nation's capital. JANAP means Joint Army-Navy-Air Publication. This means that it covers everyone in all the armed services. It plainly was issued by the Joint Chiefs of Staff; it undoubtedly originated at a higher level, probably the National Security Council or the CIA or both, jointly. (For details on the CIA activity re UFOs, see Chapter Nine.)

JANAP 146 was designed to pacify the public while the befuddled military sought some means of coping with the UFOs. Under this order the Air Force, and *only* the Air Force, was to investigate all UFO sightings and *only* the Air Force could make any public statements on the subject. Also under this order the Air Force was specifically ordered not to describe the objects as anything other than some conventional object or condition. The censorship policy did

202

not originate with the Air Force; that agency has been merely carrying out orders.

There are other censorship orders relating to this problem, but JANAP 146 was the first and still serves as a pattern for the later modifications.

The censorship of UFO information was a move of desperation, designed to bring about an official policy of "playing down" the problem while the authorities searched for the answers. It may have been a wise policy in the circumstances, but events and the passage of time have exposed it and nullified its usefulness.

13. *"What can you tell us about Project Blue Book?"*

Simply that it must operate within the restrictions imposed by the censorship regulations, which means that it is required to tell the public only that there is nothing up there, regardless of what it finds, or has found. In keeping with this policy it *classifies* all important UFO sightings—only the *unclassified* cases are available for scrutiny by newsmen and other interested parties.

Customarily, when UFOs are numerous, Project Blue Book issues another of its "statistical reports" which proclaim that the Project has investigated umpteen-thousand reports and explained away all but a few hundred cases, which it says it could not explain "due to lack of details." (In the April, 1963 issue of the *Yale Scientific Magazine,* a group of Yale mathematicians who had analyzed some of these Project Blue Book "statistical reports," damned the reports as worthless—as compilations of faulty assumptions, bad arithmetic, and false conclusions.)

As with so many others interested in the subject, I have been disturbed by the offhand manner in which the Project Blue Book reports have been dealt out to the public in times of public concern over the UFO problem. I felt that there was something basically unsound in the reports— that the premise on which they were based was at fault, and not merely the mathematics of the things.

You will notice that Blue Book came into existence in 1952. It was the publicity organization designed to carry out the systematic hoodwinking of the public required by JANAP 146. It was the mouthpiece for the censorship policy.

In order to stand a chance of being believed, Blue Book had to describe how it arrived at its alleged figures. In the March, 1967 statement by the head of the project, we are told that 11,107 sightings since 1947 have been investigated, and only 676 of them are still unexplained.

This means that Project Blue Book, since its inception in 1952, is claiming to have investigated roughly ten thousand sightings. Now these ten thousand sightings have come in from every state in the Union, including Alaska and Hawaii.

In a recent publicity photograph of the staff of Project Blue Book we are told that it consists of just FIVE (count 'em!) persons, identified as Major Hector Quintanilla, Jr., who was in charge of the project in early 1967; First Lieutenant William Marley, Jr.; Staff Sergeant Harold T. Jones; Mrs. Hilma Lewis, typist; and Mrs. Marilyn Stancombe, secretary.

The two ladies are certainly not investigators. Major Quintanilla rarely goes out on an investigation unless it looks like a very difficult case to refute (for example, the Exeter case in New Hampshire). That leaves a Staff Sergeant and a First Lieutenant to do the field work. If the case load was evenly divided by years, each man would have had to investigate three hundred thirty cases per year, scattered over at least twenty-five states. This figures out at almost a case per day—and in the years when the load was heavy, as in 1965, 1966, and 1967, the number of cases per man would be well above the three hundred thirty average.

What kind of investigation could one man do, covering that many cases and that much geography? How could he possibly travel from place to place and still find any time whatever for investigation after he got there and before he had to leave?

Under the circumstances as stated, Major Quintanilla and his two-man staff could not possibly conduct the number of investigations claimed and devote any reasonable amount of time to any case, much less to all of them. It would be a physical impossibility. They simply could not cover the territory, even if they traveled by UFO!

Project Blue Book was created and has operated as a smoke screen. It is located at Wright-Patterson Air Force Base in Dayton, Ohio. That base is also the home of the Air Technical Intelligence Center, which investigates and evaluates everything having to do with possibly alien objects in the air over the United States and its possessions.

ATIC makes no public statements.

It issues no "statistical reports" on UFOs.

ATIC does the job for which the bows are taken by Propaganda Blue Book.

14. *"How are the UFOs propelled?"*
According to Dr. Hermann Oberth, the famed German scientist who headed a commission to investigate the UFOs for West Germany, he and his colleagues had come to the conclusion that the UFOs were ". . . conceived and directed by intelligent beings of a very high order, and they

are propelled by distorting the gravitational field, converting gravity into usable energy."

If this should prove to be correct, it would be in keeping with Einstein's Unified Field Theory, which holds that gravity, magnetism, and electricity are different manifestations of the same form of energy.

Shortly after Dr. Oberth made that remarkable remark during a press conference in Europe in 1954, he was flown to the United States, put under the security muzzle, and placed on the staff at the great rocket arsenal at Huntsville, Alabama, where he worked under his famous former pupil, Dr. Werner Von Braun. In February of 1960, Dr. Oberth returned to West Germany to qualify for his pension. He held another press conference at Frankfurt when he landed at the airfield. Dr. Oberth told the newsmen that the United States had made considerable progress in unraveling the secrets of electrical propulsion, and added that by 1970 he expected to see men going to the moon in electrically driven devices. Did he mean devices with ion-propulsion systems? he was asked. Dr. Oberth was emphatic in his reply; he meant *"electrical propulsion"*—period.

If the UFOs are propelled by conversion of gravity it would simplify space travel, since it would eliminate the necessity of carrying a fuel supply. Gravity pervades the universe; where it is weakest, less of it should be needed for propulsion; where it is strongest, more of it would be available.

There is ample evidence that there is a powerful field associated with the UFOs. Countless pilots, motorists, ship's captains, and even scientists (at the South Pole in July of 1965) have witnessed and reported the effects of the UFO's electromagnetic fields on their gear and their radio,

206

radar, and ignition systems. (For detailed examples, see pages 51-63, *Flying Saucers—Serious Business.*)

True magazine reported, in January of 1966, that the United States was sponsoring forty-six different research projects which were trying to unlock the secrets of gravity.

The evidence led Dr. Oberth and his colleagues to the conclusion that the designers of the UFOs had already "unlocked the secrets of gravity." Therefore, it is not surprising to find that the United States is engaged in such a project on such a scale.

15. *"If the UFOs are really alien spacecraft, why would they land in swamps so frequently?"*

In our own plans for dealing with circumstances, if and when we reach another inhabited planet, we have already included provisions for emergency landings for inspection or repairs.

Our astronauts will be under orders to make such landings in either deserts or swamps, in order to secure the greatest possible amount of isolation.

That idea is not copyrighted. It is quite possible that the procedure we intend to follow is already in use by others.

16. *"For several years we used to hear frequently of airline pilots' reports of UFOs, but those reports are rare in recent years. Can you explain this?"*

Airline pilots made numerous and detailed reports of UFOs and, because of their exceptionally high competence as observers, their reports carried a great deal of weight.

The official military censorship order, JANAP 146, went into effect in mid-1952, as I have explained earlier. The official policy of ridiculing those who reported UFOs, and of denying the existence of the objects, drastically reduced the number of UFO reports carried by the news wires. By January of 1954, there were only two national sources of such information. One was my radio news program nightly over the Mutual Network; the other was the reports by pilots of commercial planes.

I was ousted from the network when the Pentagon began allocating lush defense contracts to the detriment of my sponsors, the American Federation of Labor. My exit plugged that source of UFO reporting.

The silencing of the airline pilots was already under way before I was muzzled. On February 17, 1954, officers of the Military Transport Intelligence met with officials of the airlines and of the Airline Pilots Association at the Roosevelt Hotel in Hollywood. The civilians present were told that the UFOs represented a serious problem for the government. The civilians representing the airlines and the pilots were asked to "cooperate."

Under the arrangements worked out at that meeting, the pilots were to radio any sightings immediately to the nearest airport control tower—*and to make no public statements about the incident.*

Later this arrangement was modified (after some of the radio reports were overheard and broadcast) and the airlines instituted a policy which required the pilot and co-pilot and the navigator, if any, to sign the report of the sighting. This led to irksome questioning by both airline and military officials, and most pilots quickly discovered that it was simpler to see nothing and say nothing.

However, pilots do occasionally report UFOs, especially if they see them outside the United States! In the *NICAP Investigator* for January, 1967, there are two such reports.

One concerns the objects reported by Captain Henrique Maia, flying a Boeing 707 into Luanda, Angola (West Africa) on Wednesday, December 7, 1966.

Captain Maia first noticed the two shiny disc-shaped things following his passenger plane when he was over the Atlantic about thirty minutes out of Luanda. He banked from side to side so his co-pilot could get a better look at the objects, as well as himself. The passengers were alerted over the intercom, and they, too, later told airport authorities and newsmen that they had seen the things "very close to the plane."

The Luanda radar informed Captain Maia that there was no other plane traffic in his area at the time of the sighting. The objects vanished back out over the ocean as the jetliner began its descent toward the airport.

Another interesting airliner encounter with a UFO involved the pilot and three crew members of a Canadian Pacific jet passenger plane, en route from Lima, Peru, to Mexico City, about 2 a.m., December 30, 1966.

According to the written report filed by Captain Robert Milbank with aeronautical authorities in Mexico City shortly after landing, this is what happened:

"The passengers were all asleep. We were flying at 35,-000 feet off the coast of Peru, just south of the equator. Time was about 2 a.m.

"The co-pilot and I saw two white lights on the horizon to the left of the DC-8. The co-pilot was John D. Dahl of White Rock, British Columbia. He notified the other crew members: Navigator Mike Mole of Mexico City, Pilot Trainee Wolfgang Poepperi and Purser Joseph Lugs. All five of us then observed the events which followed.

"The lights were close together. They were twinkling

209

and at first I thought they might be stars. But there should not have been two stars so close together.

"As we watched, the two lights seemed to be gradually separating and they were getting closer to us. If it had been a plane, I thought, the lights might have been red and white or red and green—but these lights were both white.

"Then I noticed that one of the lights was pulsating and changing in intensity. Then we noticed two beams of light coming from the lights and shining upward in a V-shape. The two main lights seemed to be descending and they levelled off alongside our aircraft. At one time the object shot out a trail of sparks, like a rocket.

"I tried to convince myself that this object was only another aircraft—or a satellite re-entering the atmosphere, but it was pretty obvious that it was neither of those.

"Then it seemed to be edging closer to us—and we could see a string of lights between the two white lights. It levelled off at our left wing tip and, in the light of the full moon, we could see a shape between the two lights, a structure which appeared to be thicker in the middle. It stayed there for a couple of minutes and then disappeared behind our aircraft."

Captain Milbank said that, while he did not believe in flying saucers, he felt that what he and his crew members had watched was a strange phenomenon which people commonly call flying saucers.

The statements by the professional fliers mentioned above, flying foreign planes and seemingly unhampered by official censorship policy, may be contrasted with this interesting experience involving American Airlines Flight No. 162, en route from San Francisco to Houston on the night of January 16, 1967.

210

The final leg of the flight was from El Paso to Houston. The plane left El Paso about 10:00 p.m. Most of the passengers had debarked at the previous stops. Only a handful were aboard the plane at the time of the incident, but among those few were two professional psychologists, Miss Teresa Trittipoe of the Manpower Development Institute, and Dr. Philip Welsh, Computer Applications.

In her report to NICAP, Miss Trittipoe states that she first noticed a brilliant point of light following the airliner and that she was attracted to it by its obvious movement among the stars. The UFO changed speed and course several times before Miss Trittipoe called it to the attention of Dr. Welsh. Together they watched it for about five minutes; they saw it moving up and down erratically, saw it approach the plane and then reverse its course.

She adds that she and the doctor watched the performance in silence, uncertain of what they were observing but totally rapt by what they felt was an impossible performance. They did not contact the few other passengers in the cabin, most of whom were either reading or sleeping. They did notice, however, that the pilot turned on his landing lights in mid-air for a few seconds, then made a sharp bank and banked again to get back on course. This would indicate that the pilot was aware of the UFO and was possibly checking for cockpit reflections. A few seconds later, according to the psychologists, the UFO duplicated the maneuvers of the plane.

When the American airliner landed at San Antonio, the witnesses report that "the UFO shot up and made a wide hyperbolic swing into the sky. . . ."

Neither the pilot nor the co-pilot made any public mention of the incident, which would have gone unreported had not Miss Trittipoe made a written account of it for

NICAP. The silence of the crew in this case may reasonably be interpreted as evidence of their realization that silence would save them a lot of trouble; it is easier to deny having seen a UFO than to be annoyed by having to explain what they had seen.

Dr. Welsh and Miss Trittipoe, both scientifically trained observers, were admittedly dumbfounded.

The crew, for a different reason, was speechless.

17. *"What kind of creatures operate the UFOs?"*

Virtually all the credible cases have described the same type of creature: small, manlike beings commonly called "humanoids"—wearing (generally) coverall type garments of white or shiny material, and ofttimes equipped with transparent helmets.

There have been a few other instances where witnesses have reported "monsters" of various description, but these are rarities.

Since it is possible that the UFOs do not all have the same origin, it is conceivable that they might contain more than one type of operator, with the humanoids predominating by a broad margin.

We must not dismiss the possibility that the so-called humanoids are not the designers or builders of the craft they operate, either. Some close-up descriptions of them mention their claws; others mention their webbed hands. We would interpret the presence of claws as prejudicial to the development of the delicate precision equipment necessary to constructing the UFOs and their components.

Therefore, it may be that the humanoids are really creatures of lower social order, capable of being trained to operate the craft but considered expendable. This would be similar to our own early experiments with chimpanzees in space shots. We had to discontinue their use when we soon discovered their limitations. But if we had small, intelligent beings capable of operating our own spacecraft without risking our astronauts on routine trips, it is conceivable that we would utilize them.

Mice and monkeys have their shortcomings.

Humanoids would be the answer—if we had them.

(The term "little green men," frequently used in oblique references to the humanoid occupants of spacecraft, seems to have originated in a science-fiction article in *Amazing Stories* magazine, published in October, 1946.

Noted psychic and author Harold Sherman in those days was writing science fiction. In that issue of *Amazing Stories* he wrote a story called "The Green Man," which purported to describe a creature from another planet who performed such prophetic acts as stopping automobiles by means of a ray from the spacecraft.

Writes Mr. Sherman: "This story, breaking a few months before the advent of 'flying saucers' over the United States, seems to have contributed to the literature of little green men from space. I believe that I was the *first* to refer to visitors from space as *green*. I followed this story with another, 'The Green Man Returns,' and the die was cast!"—F.E.)

"Tell me, Judge Crater, after all these years, how does it feel to be homeward bound?"

11

The year 1967 came in with a rush of UFO reports which amounted to a minor deluge. NICAP was receiving about one hundred reports per week as late as April; I was getting nearly as many. Neither of us was getting all of them.

There were so many reports that it would be difficult—and perhaps impossible—to include a majority of them in this book, so I shall endeavor to report a selection of what seem to be representative cases, and the more detailed.

On the night of January 17th, Francis Bedel, Jr., 23, of Portland, Indiana, was driving on State Highway 135, a two-lane blacktop road. He was north of Freetown, he later reported to State Police, when a brilliant glowing white light darted into his field of vision. It apparently hovered over the road for a few seconds, then slowly reversed its course. Bedel was so busy staring at the spectacle that he lost control of his car, which left the road and was badly damaged. State Police who investigated said that Bedel was not drinking and was not injured in the crash.

On that same stretch of highway on that same night, Mr. and Mrs. Phil Patton, of Freetown, reported to State Police that a brightly lighted disc-shaped craft came down alongside their car.

Mr. Patton told State Trooper Conrad that the object moved along the highway right in front of their car and about one hundred feet distant from it. They estimated that it was about one hundred feet above the road and they described it as circular in shape and about the size of a small house.

The Pattons reported to police that they heard no sound from the object but that its outstanding characteristic was the extreme brilliance of its lights, predominantly red but with flashing yellow and white along the side or bottom of the thing. After half a minute, it flashed up and away.

According to State Police who investigated, the description given by the Pattons was identical to that given by Francis Bedel, the young man who wrecked his car while watching a similar spectacle, about a mile from the scene of the Pattons' experience.

In the early morning hours of January 13th, dozens of police officers in Labette, Cherokee, and Crawford Counties in Kansas, also in Pittsburg and Galena, Kansas, and Joplin, Missouri, reported a strange object at very low altitude in the sky. It crossed those areas in two hours, between 4 and 6 a.m. according to the witnesses.

Lieutenant Charles Hickman of the Joplin Police Department reported that, after being alerted by the Pittsburg police, he and five other officers took up a position about four miles north of Joplin. His description tallies with that of the other police: "At first I didn't see anything but then in a few minutes I saw a huge silvery colored object, coming toward Joplin. It was traveling at not more than a thousand feet above the ground and was moving very slowly. There was no noise, no vapor trail. Just this big shining, glowing light, white in color."

No experimental balloons were in that section of the country at the time, according to authorities.

On Monday, January 9th, before the sighting just reported, two teen-age brothers, Dan Jaroslaw, 17, and Grant, 15, reported that they had photographed a strange object over Lake St. Clair, only a couple of miles from Selfridge Air Force Base. They said that they saw the thing moving slowly at very low altitude (so low that it would have been under the range of the radar at the Base, if their estimate of altitude was correct—F.E.). They asserted that the thing was in view about ten minutes in all—long enough for one of them to grab a small Polaroid camera and snap several pictures.

When United Press carried the pictures, the Air Force made an effort to get hold of the original prints. But the boys had evidently heard of the experiences of others who had surrendered their original prints or negatives to the Air Force, so they offered to give the Air Force a set of copies, but the originals were under lock and key in a bank.

Here once again the Air Force could wash its hands of a very difficult case by saying that they had no explanation because they had not examined the original material.

Dr. J. Allen Hynek was shown a set of prints from the photographs taken by the Jaroslaw brothers and he was quoted on the newswires as saying that in his opinion the pictures were genuine . . . not a hoax. And Dr. Hynek added that they resembled other UFO photographs he had seen.

"The striking thing about these pictures," said Dr. Hynek, "is the similarity these pictures have to other Air Force UFO photos I have seen and also to verbal descriptions I have taken from reliable people."

After his statement was publicized, Dr. Hynek told the news services that he had not intended to imply that the pictures taken by the Jaroslaw brothers were actual photographs of UFOs, but merely that they were actual photographs.

If you wish to conclude that between those two statements Dr. Hynek had heard from his employers at Project Blue Book, I shall be glad to join you.

At Newcastle, New South Wales, Australia, two veteran police officers reported what they called an "eerie experience" while on duty in Windale, a community about ten miles south of Newcastle.

At 3 a.m. on January 17th, according to the official report filed by Sergeant J. Bell and Constable F. Tracy, they spotted a strange object coming in from the sea at an altitude of between four hundred and six hundred feet. It was carrying two flashing red lights, and Sergeant Bell said that at intervals the red lights dimmed almost to the point of extinction and were replaced by a single but very brilliant beam of white light which projected straight forward along the line of travel. Both officers agreed that the object was traveling not faster than ten miles per hour when first seen. Both officers signed the report. They said that they had gone from their base at Charleston to Windale to make an investigation and both were out of the car when the strange craft was spotted. They said: "We saw a UFO. We both saw it at the same time. It was an eerie experience."

Milan, Indiana, made the news wires when 15-year-old Reed Thompson reported that he had taken pictures of an aerial object which was similar in description to one seen by three State Troopers in the Seymour-Bedford area, about forty miles west of Milan.

On the afternoon of January 19th, at about 3 p.m., Reed says that he heard a rumbling sound like a train. When the noise persisted, the boy says that he went to the window and was startled by a shiny object which was moving very slowly about twenty-five feet above the ground. He got his camera, a plastic job which had cost him fifty cents and the label from a can of pork and beans, and snapped several pictures of the thing. He told authorities that it appeared to be about five or six feet in diameter and four or five feet thick at the center.

His father, William Thompson, President of the Milan Furniture Company, told newsmen that he and others had questioned the boy at length and had not been able to shake his story.

The *Cairo* (Illinois) *Citizen* headlined its UFO story of January 20: UFO BRIGHTENS THE SKY IN CAIRO AREA: RESIDENTS DESCRIBE FLASHING LIGHTS.

The story noted that lighted objects which performed strangely had been causing considerable excitement for several nights in the area around Cape Girardeau, Missouri, and seemed to have crossed the river into the Cairo area on the night of January 19th. Two Cairo men, Police Officers Carl Jones and Gene Smith, heard the Sikeston, Missouri, police radio talking about the object and they drove up onto the levee at Cairo where they could get a better view.

The officers reported that the object was hovering between Cairo and Charleston (across the Mississippi River) at an altitude of between five hundred and one thousand feet. They watched it for a period of seven minutes.

Said Patrolman Smith: "It had red and white pulsating lights which changed about every five seconds to green. It hovered for several minutes, moved to the left, then moved back to its original position and then dropped to

221

ground level and vanished. If Carl Jones hadn't been with me I would never have said a word about it. You would have thought I was nuts!"

That was about 6:30 p.m. At 2 a.m. the following morning C. E. Stout, a correspondent for the Cairo paper, reported that he and a group of friends had watched a strange performance of a light which flashed white, green, red, and amber. It hovered over a house where the group was gathered, on the road between Thebes and McClure. The witnesses watched the UFO for about forty-five minutes. They report that after it had hovered directly overhead for a few minutes it moved rapidly toward the east, stopped, returned, and was last seen moving southward down the Mississippi River.

At Granite City, Illinois, which is across the river from the north edge of St. Louis, police watched an object with flashing lights which, as Patrolman Everett Kelley said: "Made a believer out of me!"

It was first spotted about 3 o'clock Saturday morning (January 28th) by Officer Ralph Parmley. He radioed that he was watching "a ball of light that changed from red to blue to red" hanging in the northwest sky. He said that it was close enough that he could see that it had a kind of dome on top and a bottom segment that looked like— "an inverted cup or a shallow bowl, upside down."

Police Officers Bill Harris, Robert Astorian, Al Young, Glen Wright, and Allen LeMaster, along with Madison County Deputy Sheriff Delbert Clemmons, all observed the object through binoculars. They too saw the shape reported by Patrolman Parmley.

"It acted sort of unusual," said Patrolman Kelley, and Sergeant Harold Mitchell concurred. "It moved down suddenly, then to the right and then down again before it vanished."

It is quite possible that the trite explanation for such things may be true—in some cases. Some of these sightings which aroused so much interest and attracted so much attention during January of 1967 may indeed have been the planet Venus. But there were many sightings, then and later, which could not have been Venus because of the time at which they were seen, the movements of the object, and the directions in which they were seen. Venus is very bright, but she is also very stable. Her location is well known and she can be depended upon not to go roaming around, changing course, and chasing automobiles.

January of the new year marched off the calendar in a blaze of flashing lights from all directions of the compass. And February took up where its predecessor had left off. The scene shifts to Erlanger, Kentucky. The time, 8:55 p.m.

Mr. J. C. Ilg, a tax clerk for the Brotherhood of Railway Clerks, and his wife were driving north on the Dixie Highway. As they drove between Erlanger and Lookout Heights their attention was attracted by a pair of large bright white lights ahead and well above the car.

Mr. Ilg reported: "As we moved closer the lights seemed to change position and move farther apart. They appeared to be moving as though they were a part of the same object, although at that point we could not make out any shape behind them."

They agreed that the thing had the white lights on opposite sides, or ends.

"Norma saw a red light in the middle of it, larger than the white lights on the ends," Mr. Ilg said.

"Then, as the thing moved in a northwesterly direction, we could both see that it had four window-like lights on the bottom of it. Understand now, the front and rear white lights, the little windows and the red light all seemed to be part of the same craft, whatever it was."

The object seemed to hover briefly from time to time and finally disappeared behind the hills in the northwest. It was the fourth sighting of a similar object in Kentucky in ten days. On the preceding week, three sightings were reported from just one county, Shelby.

Ralph Ditter of Zanesville, Ohio, photo enthusiast, amateur astronomer, and by trade a barber, made headlines on February 7th when he finally released for publication some Polaroid pictures of an object which he said he had snapped on the preceding November 13th.

"It was a nice Sunday afternoon so I decided to go and take pictures of some furniture that my brother-in-law had built into his house, about three blocks from where I live," said Mr. Ditter.

"I was carrying a Polaroid camera. At the end of the driveway I stopped and turned around and then I saw it.

"The thing was directly over my house, about forty-seven feet in the air, and rotating slowly counter-clockwise. It was moving about ten or fifteen miles per hour.

"I took three pictures. One of them, with a filter on the lens, was underexposed. As I watched, the object drifted off to the southwest and disappeared over a hill."

He estimated the object to have been about twenty feet in diameter and said it seemed to have no effect on anything on the ground over which it moved. He let his wife and two children see the pictures and then displayed them in his barbershop but declined to have them published for fear of possible ridicule.

The pictures finally got published after NICAP member Dr. Benjamin Gilliotte of Zanesville, a former Army Air Corps officer, induced Ditter to submit prints to NICAP and to United Press.

Just south of Sandusky, Ohio, is an installation of the National Aeronautics and Space Administration, where research toward peaceful use of atomic energy is conducted. It is officially known as the Plum Brook Facility.

At 3:40 a.m. on February 10th, Perkins Township Patrolman Gary Butler reported he was patrolling alone in his car on Schenk Road when he glanced toward the NASA atomic facility and got the shock of his life, a blue-glowing disc-shaped thing which appeared to be hovering right above the plant.

It appeared to be about forty feet above the ground, and he estimated that it was from twenty to twenty-five feet in diameter.

Said Officer Butler:

"It scared me at first. I jammed on the brakes and stopped to watch it. I watched it for four or five minutes before I radioed to the Sheriff's office. That thing was real bright and there was a bluish light shining down from it."

By the time the Sheriff's Deputy arrived on the scene, the glowing disc had disappeared behind some trees— "without a sound!"—Butler reported.

Billy Neacock, reporting to the *Fairbanks Miner* from Point Barrow, Alaska, told the paper that on February 12th and 13th there was considerable UFO activity at that northernmost community on the continent.

Neacock and Sam Talaak, a member of the Barrow Village Council, told the *Fairbanks Miner* that a UFO landed on the ice of the Arctic Ocean, just offshore from Barrow, and also hovered over the theater, the dance hall, and the

Bureau of Indian Affairs buildings. Some residents reported three of the objects hovering at the same time over the theater. It may be significant that the generators at the Barrow power plant ceased to function for about one hour while the UFOs were reportedly hovering over the community. The maintenance supervisor at the generating plant said that nothing was wrong with the generators—except that they just refused to function for an hour or so.

Sam Talaak reports that the UFO he saw was in the sky south of Barrow about 6:50 p.m. moving slowly westward and occasionally dipping straight down. When it landed on the ice it was reportedly seen by many persons, including both Neacock and Talaak, but they said that it was impossible to determine its exact shape because of the brilliant light it emitted, largely orange and yellows.

If this was Venus, it must be one of the few times that planet has landed on the Arctic Ocean.

Near Goddard, Kansas, twelve miles west of Wichita, on the night of February 9th, fifteen persons watched a strange multicolored object that appeared to hang motionless in the sky for more than an hour. According to Wes Herbert, night manager for the Lincoln Oil Company, the thing sent down an intensely brilliant beam of red light at one point in the incident.

The *Topeka Daily Capital* reports that on the night of February 16th Colonel Walter Pittman and his wife and mother-in-law were returning from a movie at Forbes Air Force Base when they spotted a bright object, stationary in the sky at an altitude of about five hundred feet above highway U.S. 470, in southwest Topeka.

The mother-in-law was the first to spot the fire dripping from the bottom of the object, Colonel Pittman reported.

"Then I saw it," he said. "It looked like white phosphorus."

The trio watched the thing for about four minutes altogether, until it dimmed out, suddenly brightened again, and then blacked out completely.

Police who checked with Forbes Air Force Base were told that no flares had been dropped that night and that no UFOs had been detected by the radar.

Two patrolmen on the campus police force of Eastern Michigan University at Ypsilanti reported a bizarre sight on February 16th.

Patrolman Alfred Rogers, 48, a retired Army officer, reported that he and Officer John Markwell spotted an orange-colored object moving northeast at 9:40 p.m. Since the wind was blowing *from* that direction, the police ruled out the possibility that they were watching some kind of balloon.

The official report says:

"Object was moving in northeast direction. It was orange in color. Light seemed to be very bright. Object's duration at peak brilliance was about ten minutes. When it reached this peak it would eject a stream of fire from underneath and then the main portion would snuff out."

The first object was sighted at 9:40 p.m. Thursday, and the last two were seen at 1:15 a.m. Friday. Six officers from the Ypsilanti Police Department were on hand when the last two objects sailed over the darkened college campus, moving silently against the wind at an estimated five to ten miles per hour.

Said the police report:

"The objects (two) appeared to be flying in a formation, one a little bit higher than the first one, maybe 500 feet off the ground."

227

On the morning of February 17th, the *Watertown* (New York) *Times* was able to confirm to NICAP that their office had received a UFO report the night before which had been verified by New York State Police. Watertown is about sixty miles north of Syracuse. The scene of the sighting was Massena, New York, about seventy-five miles north and slightly east of Watertown.

The Massena police received a call from a lady who reported a bright, orange-red object "as big as a soft-ball" moving slowly across the sky. Two State Troopers were sent to investigate; they reported that they were seeing the same thing.

A third State Trooper, near Norfolk, about ten miles south of Massena, also saw the thing as it hovered over a home. He subsequently questioned the occupants of the house and found them badly frightened by the strange orange-red illumination which had accompanied the UFO.

On that same night of February 16th, while the State Troopers around Massena, New York, were watching a glowing orange gob of light, Mrs. Esther Millard of Bandon, Oregon, was watching something similar. But she got close enough, she reported to police, to see the shape of the object which carried the light.

Mrs. Millard, owner of the Millard School, said that she was taking her German shepherd dog for a walk at about 10:20 p.m. As she turned the corner she noticed a glowing red-orange light hanging just above the school gymnasium, about fifty feet above the ground and not more than one hundred fifty feet from where she stood.

She reported to Chief of Police D. S. MacDonald that she could see that the light was actually on the bottom of a rectangular object about seven feet wide and possibly fifteen feet tall. It moved in an upright position, tilted slightly forward.

Mrs. Millard said that when she first saw the object she thought that it was going to land on the roof of the gymnasium. It was quite low—below the level of the tree tops. After remaining virtually motionless for several minutes the object rose swiftly and silently, crossed Bradley Lake, and was last seen flying high over the ocean.

The following day, police checked with students at the school and learned that several of them had seen a similar object the previous night but had been afraid to report it.

Among the credible witnesses we might include the editor of the *Frostburg* (Maryland) *Citizen,* who describes in a front-page story in the issue of March 9th the brilliant object which he and some other residents of the area observed.

Editor Fred Rosenbaum, Mrs. Rosenbaum, Jack Spiker, and Robert Stahl, all watched the light for about forty-five minutes. It lasted much too long for a flare, gradually changed color from white to pink to red as it seemed to be moving away.

Mrs. Rosenbaum reports that she received a call on the evening of March 8th from Jack Spiker at 7 p.m., alerting her to the spectacle in the sky. She had heard of such things being seen in the area and had borrowed a pair of 10-power binoculars . . . just in case. When Spiker called, she grabbed the binoculars and hurried outside. It took only a few seconds to get focused on the glowing object. Mrs. Rosenbaum, her husband, and Jack Spiker (who also had binoculars) agreed that the object was bobbing and weaving about in the sky, that it was cigar shaped, and that it had red flames jetting out from the sides of the craft.

229

Another oddity in this case which the witnesses noted was that there was a plane in the vicinity. They could clearly discern the shape of the plane as well as that of the UFO. When the plane turned in the direction of the UFO, the UFO blinked out and did not reappear until the plane was in another part of the sky.

"Then," says Mrs. Rosenbaum, "it would again become visible, dimly at first, brightening gradually until it reached full brilliance. It did this five or six times as we watched."

The thing seemed to be doing a wild dance in the air. It was weaving and bobbing, as seen in the binoculars. Was this an optical illusion created by the movement of the glasses? Fortunately, the witnesses turned their instruments on stars. The stars were steady points of light—but the cigar-shaped UFO was unmistakably doing a gyrating dance of some sort.

Says Mrs. Rosenbaum: "It was really beautiful. It was the most beautiful brilliant red and white light I have ever seen."

Newspaper Editor Tom Dreiling of the *Goodland* (Kansas) *Daily News,* was one of the witnesses to a bizarre incident which, like the things reported by the Frostburg, Maryland, editor, was well described by credible observers. It, too, was seen on the night of March 8th.

Many persons in and near Sharon Springs and Atwood called police to report that they were watching the maneuvers of a strangely lighted object at very low altitude. Sharon Springs Sheriff G. L. Sullivan and Police Chief Al Kisner decided to check out a call from a personal friend who was reportedly watching the thing hovering at a point estimated to be about fifteen miles north of Sharon

Springs. The two officers drove north about twenty miles before they, too, saw the object.

They described it as about twelve to fourteen feet long, spherical, and with an object attached to the bottom of the craft which was circular and about twelve feet in diameter. The UFO was not more than one hundred fifty to two hundred feet above the ground. It was carrying three lights: red, green, and amber.

The officers watched the thing for several minutes, during which time it made two descents and shot upward again to its former altitude, finally moving away to the northeast.

When the same, or a similar craft, returned to Goodland around 2 a.m., the police alerted Editor Tom Dreiling, who accompanied Patrolman Ron Weehunt, and the two of them were among the numerous witnesses of the strange object. They saw it move westward across the town, then change course and return eastward across the town, and finally disappear from sight, still at low altitude, in the direction of Colby, where police and others confirmed by telephone that they had spotted the craft and were watching it as it moved over that town.

The descriptions all tallied closely, and the *Goodland Daily News* carried a sketch based on details furnished by witnesses.

The *Honolulu Advertiser* headlined: TWO UFOS SPOTTED IN SKIES OVER HAWAII as an eight-column banner front-page story in its issue of January 23, 1967.

The paper reports that at least seven police officers, the officers and crew of a ship at sea, and several commercial pilots reported Unidentified Flying Objects over Oahu on the previous day.

231

First reported about 5:50 a.m. by two police officers at Keeomaku and Malakoa streets, the thing was described as a brilliant yellow thing, encircled by a bluish mist or glow which was about one hundred times the diameter of the yellow light. It was moving from Koko Head toward Ewa, during the six minutes it was in view. It left no vapor trail, said the officers, but the blue misty effect definitely traveled with the object.

A few minutes later, the second UFO appeared, at 6:03, according to the *Honolulu Advertiser* and the police records. This time there were two bright lights at great altitude, hovering over Koko Head after moving west to east, opposite to the direction of the first object, according to the witnesses, which included numerous police officers.

A policeman in Waikiki radioed at 6:20 that he had spotted the objects and that a jet plane was trying to close with them. At 6:28 he radioed to headquarters that one jet was near the lights and that other jets were approaching.

A ship at sea also radioed that it was watching the same aerial show. Honolulu Police Headquarters notified the Honolulu Airport Control Tower, the Air Force UFO Section, the U.S. Weather Bureau, the Hawaiian Air Defense Division, and State Civil Defense.

The official explanations were manifold and transparent. One object, said the Air Force at Hickam Field, was in reality "possibly" a rocket launched from Vanderburg Air Force Base in California.

The other objects, seen a few minutes later, were "probably" the star Antares.

And the jets which were seen were "possibly" commercial aircraft.

And the official explanations, which were ruled out by

many of the known facts in the case, were undoubtedly pure swamp gas.

On that same evening of January 22nd, police in Houston, Texas, were the recipients of an admitted eight reports of a fast-moving UFO—reports which came from all parts of the city.

Among the witnesses was Dr. Albert Kuntz, psychologist at the University of Houston, who told authorities that he and a neighbor watched the antics of the UFO for more than thirty minutes. He described it as resembling a boomerang, carrying a red light or lights.

"It darted about the sky. It stopped. It retraced its flight path. It was erratic in terms of the movement it made."

The sightings ended when the sky became overcast, about 8:30, according to the *Houston Post*.

The *Houston Tribune* devoted its front page on February 23rd to a headline and a huge drawing of a UFO.

SAUCERS BUZZ WHARTON TREETOPS; CONVERT SKEPTICS TO UFO WATCH—Below that was a large drawing of the object involved, which the text beneath the picture explained was "—a composite description of what dozens of residents in the Wharton area reported seeing this week from distances ranging from sixty yards away to aerial maneuvers high in the sky. Closest observers included three bankers, a newspaper editor, a radio station owner and a school teacher, who said 'the craft was fifty to sixty feet in diameter, made no sound as it flew, and executed maneuvers defying all known laws of aerodynamics.'"

Wharton is about forty-five miles southwest of Houston. El Campo is about nine miles southwest of Wharton. Bay City, the other community involved, is twenty-five miles south of Wharton, on the Colorado River.

One of the witnesses, Frank Jones, is editor of the *Wharton Journal*. He points out that there are some highly strategic installations in that area. "Nine miles south of El Campo is an unusually large radar installation operated by M.I.T., at Danevang," he said. "It has been rumored that the station is operating on a 24-hour basis, bouncing radar beams off the sun and the moon, but of course this has not been confirmed."

Jones reports that he joined a party of several persons who were already watching a strange spectacle in the sky. It included K. R. Miller, 33, department store manager, and his wife, who first spotted a UFO as they were driving home from church on Sunday evening, February 19th.

Mr. Miller told authorities that when he realized that the pulsating red light was closing fast and losing altitude, he pulled off the highway and jumped out of his car.

"It was coming in fast and was at about telephone-pole height. The thing crossed the highway in front of my car about 60 yards from us, just high enough to clear the trees.

"It was a huge craft," he added. "It must have been 50 to 60 feet in diameter and was circular-shaped. My wife and I could see a band of colored lights—red, amber, blue and green, encircling the lower portion of the craft. It was either bell-shaped or like a saucer with a dome; we could not tell exactly because of the brilliance of a glaring white light in the upper portion of the superstructure.

"Then I saw two more similar lights hovering in the distance. I barreled into Lane City and called Frank Jones, editor of the *Wharton Journal*."

Mr. Miller, a four-year veteran of the Air Force, is familiar with known aircraft designs, including helicopters. The objects they were watching along the highway that memorable Sunday night were none of these, he declared.

"These things were unlike anything I had ever seen. The one which passed over the highway made no noise, not even a rush of air, although it must have been traveling at 75 miles an hour.

"I could definitely see a large lighted window or portal of some sort in the upper portion, above the rotating lights on the craft," Miller added.

By the time Frank Jones reached the scene, the astounded Millers had been joined by Lane City Mayor Melvin Weaver, Jr., and Marlowe Preston, publisher of the *Wharton Journal*. This group, and Jones, all watched an unusual lighted object hovering over the sulphur plant at New Gulf, about five miles away. It was joined by several other lights and then the objects accelerated suddenly and began gyrating erratically over the plant for several minutes.

Editor Frank Jones reports:

"I told them it was only a bright star—but suddenly it shot forward with a tremendous burst of speed, stopped dead still, hung for a while, then shot upward at a 90-degree angle. Then it dropped back down to where it had been before.

"Through my binoculars I could see the red and white lights of other objects as they moved—could see them clearly. They could easily have been mistaken for aircraft unless you watched them for a while and saw the terrific movements and maneuvers—aerobatics—as if they were showing off."

It was later learned that Marlowe Preston, Jr. and Jay Harrison were watching from the studios of KANI, near Wharton.

John Wilson, 45, is President of the Wharton Bank and Trust. He is also a veteran of the Air Force in World War

II, having served four years as a navigator. He told the *Houston Tribune* that he got a good look at one of the UFOs through the binoculars. He said he could clearly distinguish the stacks at the sulphur plant over which the UFO was operating.

"It was definitely a craft of some sort. Circular shaped and of a metallic-silvery appearance. It gave off a greenish blue glow, at times tinged with red.

"It appeared to be stationary above the stacks, then it would suddenly zoom diagonally upward. There did not seem to be any angle or any degree of sudden turn that it could not perform."

While the banker and editor and the others were watching the UFOs from the highway, says the *Houston Tribune*, a family about a fourth of a mile away, on the banks of the Colorado River, was having a nerve-shattering experience.

It was the home of Sipirano Barron. From the reports made by the witnesses to authorities later, a UFO which seemed to be out of control, skimmed in from the southwestern sky, and literally jarred the house.

Barron, a rice farmer, told authorities that he and his three children had witnessed the object gliding downward across the river, spitting white flames and listing badly on one side. As the trio watched, two more of the objects came streaking in, evidently following the first craft.

By using a sixty-foot-high tree as a reference point, Barron estimated that the object was at about two hundred feet altitude when first seen; he also calculated that it was about fifty feet in diameter. A fraction of a second after it dropped from sight behind the trees and the river bank, there was a brilliant flash. The ensuing roar jarred the Barrons' home, causing doors to fly open and glasses to rattle throughout the building.

Two hours prior to the uproar near the Barron home, other witnesses reported strange spectacles nearby.

A school teacher, the wife of Editor Frank Jones, told authorities that she was one of those who watched a pulsing red light come in at treetop level over the airstrip at a small field on Bowling Lane Road. She says: "It ran the full length of the field in between the two rows of landing lights along the strip. It stopped at the end of the runway and reversed its direction in the twinkling of an eye and shot back in the direction from which it came."

Bank Vice President George Scheel viewed the object through binoculars.

"With the naked eye you could only see a moving red light," said Scheel, "but through the binoculars you could see that it resembled two incandescent platters, inverted and stuck together at the rims."

One of the most interesting incidents from the UFO flap of 1967 came from South Hill, Virginia. Mr. C. N. Crowder, Manager of the Mobile Chemical Company, made the report to authorities.

Crowder told police that he left the company warehouse about 9 p.m. on April 21st. As he came around a bend in the blacktop highway, he discovered a roadblock in the form of an object which "resembled a metal storage tank, at least twelve feet in diameter and standing on legs about three feet high. It was astraddle of the road."

The witness estimated that the object was possibly 17 feet in height. He saw no windows or other details—just that tanklike object blocking the road.

When he got to a point about 200 feet from the thing, he flashed on his bright lights.

"Just about that time, the thing shot out a tremendous

237

burst of white-looking fire from the bottom of the object and it went straight up.

"In a flash it was gone, but with my bright lights on I got a good look at it. It was from 15 to 20 feet tall, on legs about 3½ feet high. The blast from the bottom of it set fire to the blacktop."

When police returned to the scene with Crowder, they found a burned area about 3 feet by 2½ feet which was still warm to the touch. The following morning a search disclosed four holes broken through the blacktop, forming a rectangle about 16 feet long. The holes were about ¾ of an inch in depth and ½ an inch wide.

The official investigator on this case was an assistant to Dr. J. Allen Hynek at Northwestern University, William Powers, who heads the electronics systems at Dearborn Observatory.

Powers, assisted by some State Police officers, tried to duplicate the burn on the blacktop by igniting gasoline and kerosene. Their efforts were unsuccessful. Powers noted that the kerosene did not light readily and burned in streaks. The gasoline, he said, gave off black smoke instead of the white fumes Crowder described, and burned much longer than Crowder had estimated the original blast.

(Powers took some samples from the burned area for analysis by the chemical experts at Wright-Patterson Field, in Dayton. NICAP investigators Gordon Lore, Donald Berliner and Lee Katchen also took some samples of the same material for analysis by NICAP scientists. The NICAP investigators were first on the scene, arriving less than 24 hours after the incident was reported to police.)

When Powers had concluded his official visit to the scene of this bizarre incident, he told the *South Hills Enterprise:*

"Crowder is telling exactly what he saw and there is no reason to disbelieve him. However, I cannot account for what he saw."

Interestingly, on the same night that Crowder reported the thing which blocked and burned the road in Virginia, a very similar incident was reported to authorities in Euphrata, Washington. The terrified witnesses, who live in Kent, Wash., told the Sheriff at Euphrata that they came upon this huge and apparently metallic thing sitting in the road, and barely missed ramming it before it took off. Their description of what they saw closely parallels the thing which blocked the highway near South Hills, Virginia, as described by C. N. Crowder—with the exception that the Euphrata, Washington, object did not burn the road.

On the day following these two weird cases, Dr. James McDonald again lowered the boom on the Air Force for the manner in which it has, in his opinion, dealt with the investigation of UFO reports.

Dr. McDonald is Senior Physicist in the Institute of Atmospheric Physics at the University of Arizona. For about a year he has been investigating the UFO phenomenon, and its possible relation to meteorology, on a grant from the University. This work has taken him to Dayton, Ohio, three times for conferences with officials of Project Blue Book, examination of the Project records and examination of the Project methods.

On April 22nd, Dr. McDonald addressed the American Society of Newspaper Editors in Washington, D.C., on the subject of UFOs.

Dr. McDonald told the newsmen's convention that his own study of hundreds of outstanding UFO reports, plus

239

his personal interviews with many key witnesses in important sightings cases, has led him to the conclusion that the UFO problem is one of exceedingly great scientific importance.

"Instead of deserving the description of 'nonsense problem' which it has had during twenty years of official mishandling," said Dr. McDonald, "it warrants the attention of science, press and public, not merely within the United States, but throughout the world, as a serious problem of first-order importance."

He then dealt with what he called "the curious manner" in which the problem has been "kept out of sight and maintained in disrepute." He attributed the basic responsibility for this systematic misrepresentation to Project Blue Book, which he asserted has conducted its affairs over the past 15 years in what he denounced as "a quite superficial and incompetent manner."

He charged that since 1953, when the official policy of "playing down" the UFOs and ridiculing the witnesses took effect, Project Blue Book had been staffed with officers who had little or no scientific competence. These unqualified staffers, said Dr. McDonald, have been "explaining" most of the sighting reports *with no investigation whatever.*

"Years of Air Force assurances have kept the public, the press, Congress, and the scientific community under the impression that the UFO problem was being studied with thoroughness and scientific expertise. This I have found to be completely false.

"It is urged that the time is due—overdue—for a full-scale Congressional investigation of the UFO problem, an investigation in which the persons *outside* of the official Air Force channels can put on record the astounding history of the manner in which a problem of potentially enormous scientific importance has been swept under the rug to ridicule and misrepresentation for two decades.

"The hypothesis that the UFOs might be extra-terrestrial probes, despite its seemingly low *a priori* probability, is suggested as the least unsatisfactory hypothesis for explaining the now-available evidence."

Dr. McDonald's conclusions, based on his sincere personal efforts to ascertain *all* the facts, demonstrate once again the folly of relying on the statistics and files of Project Blue Book. He interviewed many of the persons involved in some of the major cases and found significant differences between what happened—and what the official files claimed.

His conclusions, as expressed to the editors' convention, emphasize the fact that in the field of UFO research there is no such thing as an *informed skeptic*.

The top scientific advisor on UFOs to the Air Force called for a massive computer analysis of "flying saucer" reports and of early-warning radar network trackings of the objects. Dr. J. Allen Hynek made those surprisingly frank demands to a scientific seminar at Goddard Space Flight Center. (The speech was reported in detail in *Electronic News* for January 16, 1967.)

He also told the scientists that he knew of many cases where the military early-warning radar networks had picked up and tracked UFOs; in one case, he said, the Strategic Air Command radar had tracked a UFO on a wildly erratic flight at speeds up to four thousand miles per hour.

Not only have they been tracked by radar on countless occasions, Dr. Hynek told the fellow scientists, but they have also been photographed by the worldwide optical tracking network of the International Geophysical Year (IGY). But the military made no serious effort to cope

241

with either the radar sightings or the IGY pictures. "If the military was so indifferent," Dr. Hynek asked, "then how effective are their networks for the avowed purpose of warning against unidentified aircraft?" He added that in one case, to his personal knowledge, jets were scrambled to investigate a UFO, but he did not believe there was a serious follow-up.

At the time that he made this interesting statement Dr. Hynek may have been aware that our tracking agencies, including NORAD, had been concealing for months the fact that they were tracking at least three unknown objects, which they had first picked up on their radars and cameras in May, 1966.

From May to October, government officials debated what to do about admitting publicly that they were tracking objects of unknown nature and origin, orbiting the earth.

The existence of these unknowns made headlines shortly after Dr. Hynek's talk to the Goddard Space Flight Center in the first 1967 issue of the *Satellite Situation Report* on January 20th.

Dr. Hynek told the scientific seminar at Goddard that there are four possibilities of UFO origin:

That they are secret weapons of some nation on Earth. He ruled this out on the logical basis that no nation could have kept such a project secret since 1946, and because no nation which possessed such a radically improved device would risk exposure of its secret by sending it over seventy other nations, where it could be forced down or shot down. Nor would any nation with such a technological improvement be wasting time, money, and lives on rockets and planes for high-speed travel.

242

Nor is it true that most sightings are by cranks or the gullible. In fact, said Dr. Hynek, a very high percentage are detailed reports by competent and credible observers, and these reports cannot easily be explained away.

Dr. Hynek discounted the theory that UFOs are of extraterrestrial origin. For one thing, he said, the great distances between the stars would make interstellar travel difficult if not impossible. And he went on to say that it was "virtually impossible" for high forms of life to exist on any of the other planets in our solar system. (Unless, of course, they had established bases there—exactly as we plan to do!—F.E.)

That left Dr. Hynek with but one other choice: that the UFOs are what he called "a unique natural phenomenon." On the off chance that that might be the answer, the Air Force scientific advisor recommended to the seminar that a scientific study of the problem be made by computer, to determine whether any patterns of behavioral characteristics could be determined.

All of which leaves us wondering why, if he really thinks these things are merely some form of "unique natural phenomenon" there should be such a rush to process their details with computers. If he really believes that they are such mundane objects, then there is nothing at all to fear from them and no reason at all to be in a hurry to subject them to lengthy and scientific study. If that is the correct category for the UFOs, then they fall into the classification of such other little-understood phenomena as ball lightning and will o' the wisps—interesting but harmless.

However, if they are not merely a form of natural phenomena—as the evidence leads many students of the subject to conclude—then there is every reason to be concerned about the objects, and every reason to recommend a thorough and intensive study by scientists, as Dr. Hynek has done repeatedly in recent months.

And since he has had access to the material in the possession of the military, it should not be unreasonable to conclude that he knows what he is talking about, and that he knows *why* there is a real urgency for the action he recommends.

In assessing scientific public statements of this type it must be kept in mind that scientists, too, have to observe the amenities of their profession. They must remind their listeners that it would apparently be impossible for a high-level intelligence to exist on any of the other planets in our solar system. This is pure assumption, based on some sketchy information. It will continue to be just that until we have been able to explore the planets.

And to say that the distances are too great for travel is again an assumption, predicated on the standards of man on Earth. It may not be true for other beings, elsewhere.

Scientists speculate that there must be many planets with living creatures on them. It would be more remarkable if there were none, than if they do exist.

If the living beings postulated in their scientific speculations do exist, there is a strong possibility that they may have different shapes than we have, and different life spans. To a race with a life span of a thousand of our years, a trip of twenty, or even fifty, years would not be much of an obstacle. Nor do we know whether they have entered our solar system by instrumented probes, followed by manned craft in relays from bases in space.

One of the major problems in evaluating the possibility that the UFOs may be of extraterrestrial origin is the tendency to equate everything in terms of human limitations and of human experience—and these may prove to be a pair of misleading factors when the facts are in.

Dr. J. Allen Hynek, who has had access to the facts, told that scientific seminar that it was high time that science took cognizance of the UFO problem. This view is shared by the scientists and retired military leaders at NICAP, and for the same reasons. They feel, as Dr. Hynek may feel, that the UFOs warrant more serious consideration; that they are not a military problem, but a scientific problem, and a very important problem.

Perhaps because they are not under the military regulation which limits the discussion of the UFOs, NICAP's scientists do NOT discount the extraterrestrial origin of UFOs, but openly favor it.

The last week of April brought an interesting and long-awaited admission from Soviet Russia: that they too had had their troubles with UFOs and that they were making them the object of scientific study.

Dr. Felix Zigel, an astronomer who has been connected with the Soviet space work for years, said in a magazine article in Moscow that Soviet radars have been tracking UFOs for the past twenty years, and that the Soviet scientists are as puzzled by the phenomena as their counterparts in the United States.

He also revealed that in the early years of the UFO problem, 1946-1950, the Russians suspected that they might be some sort of U.S. secret device, at the same time that we suspected that they might have been Russian. But no one now holds the idea that these might be of earthly origin, he said.

Because of the evidence which has been collected during the twenty-one-year activities of the UFOs, said Dr. Zigel, the Soviet scientific community is generally of the opinion that they are intelligently conceived and directed craft, which may come from—or operate out of—bases on Mars, since they seem to be most numerous here when Earth is making a near-approach to Mars.

Like many American scientists, Dr. Zigel called for "a thorough scientific exploration to determine, once and for all, the true origin of UFOs."

* * * * *

A commercial airline pilot, who prefers to remain anonymous, had just concluded a tour of duty and was driving to his home in an exclusive residential community a few miles northeast of Indianapolis. The time was about 11:15 p.m., May 15th, 1967.

As he turned into the lane that led to his house, he noticed a strangely lighted craft in the sky. It was moving slowly toward the south, crossing some fields behind his house at an altitude of about one thousand feet, he estimated. The thing that attracted his attention was the lighting arrangement of the object; a brilliant white light in front, a rapidly blinking red light on the rear, and pulsating red lights from front to back underneath what seemed to be a cigar-shaped craft.

The pilot phoned the airport control tower. Did they have anything on their scope in his area?

The radar man assured him that they did indeed have an unidentified object on the scope—had been watching it for several minutes.

The pilot inquired if either of the Goodyear "blimps" was up?

Neither. The radar man said he could clearly see both "blimps" tied down on the airport, only a couple of hundred yards from his position. And he added that there were no planes in that area, and no weather balloons.

The pilot reported to the Marion County Sheriff's office.

That office broadcast an alert. The dispatcher in the sheriff's office contacted the radar room at the Municipal Airport and was told that they were watching an unidentified return on the scope from an object moving about at very low altitude in the area indicated.

Two deputies who answered from the general area of the pilot's home were dispatched to the scene to check the report. The first to reach the scene was Deputy Kenneth Toler, who told me:

"It was a sight—a very strange sight. The light on the front end was brilliant. We (the pilot and the deputy) could see the shape of the thing—like a fat cigar about forty to fifty feet long, we estimated. It was moving slowly against the wind. The row of lights along the bottom was unusual—I never saw a craft with lights like that.

"We watched the thing for about 25 minutes, altogether. It was somewhere beyond a mile from us. When it got ready to leave it just took off at a steep angle. It went fast—very fast. It was out of sight in a few seconds, still rising."

This sighting is noteworthy because of the calibre of the witnesses: a commercial pilot, a deputy sheriff and the radar operator who confirmed the visual sighting with his instrument.

". . . attributable to swamp gas and other like phenomena creating illusions which to the untrained seem. . . ."

12

"Sooner or later America's astronauts are going to run into astronauts from another planet outside our solar system.

"Taking the most pessimistic figures, there would be about 1,500 planets in our galaxy which would have conditions very similar to ours. They should have animal or human life."

The speaker was the noted German science writer and educator, Willy Ley. He was addressing students and faculty of the College of Engineering and the student chapter of the American Institute of Aeronautics and Astronautics, at Virginia Tech in mid-December, 1966.

Coming from such a source, the statement is of unusual interest: "Sooner or later American astronauts are going to run into astronauts from another planet outside our solar system."

The question which comes to mind is—have they already done so?

There is the very strange case of one of our early astronauts who became unduly excited about something during the course of his orbiting. His radio messages were cut off the intercom for several minutes, lest the newsmen hear what it was that he was describing. He was brought down sooner than had been anticipated. The excitement had induced certain biological functions which threatened to become troublesome.

He was never sent aloft again.

Something exceedingly disturbing had so affected this well-trained astronaut that his reports had to be censored and his career in space had to be aborted. It should be noted that in subsequent years there was no trace of the ailment which was given out as the official cause of his problem.

Could he have seen the operator of a UFO at close range?

According to the *Air Technical Intelligence Journal* for September, 1953, he could have. For in that issue the *Journal* carried drawings of the new-type UFOs being reported as replacing the disc or so-called "flying saucer" type. And this new convex UFO shown in the *Air Force Technical Intelligence Journal* to alert the readers of that publication, clearly had a small transparent dome in the top and center of the craft, unmistakably for the use of an operator.

Had such a craft approached the astronaut of this discussion he could easily have seen the operator at close range and with the reaction known to have occurred.

There has been no official admission that *any* of our astronauts have seen either the UFOs or their operators while in orbit. But the evidence is there, and can be (and some of it—at least—has been) ferreted out.

About two hundred persons in the Muchea Tracking Station just a short distance from Perth, Australia, confirmed Major Gordon Cooper's sighting of a "greenish, glowing, disc-shaped thing" which was approaching his capsule *from the east,* a direction which no manmade device follows. (See Chapter Ten.)

"Bogey" is the term used by military fliers to indicate unidentified aircraft.

On the second orbit of Gemini 7, over Antigua, in the Leeward Islands, Astronaut Frank Borman reported that he and his companion, James A. Lovell, Jr., had sighted a bogey, above and to the left of the spacecraft, "about ten o'clock high!"

The two obviously excited astronauts were promptly assured by the officials at the Space Center that they were watching nothing more interesting than a burned-out booster rocket. Borman promptly replied that it could not possibly be a booster rocket, because he was seeing the booster separately and clearly "as a brilliant body tumbling in the brilliant sunlight." The bogey was a different object in a different part of the sky, unlike anything the men had seen before. The men also reported that several miles ahead of their Gemini capsule, and across its line of flight, they could see hundreds of small glittering objects.

Astronaut James Lovell reported that the Gemini was struck by something during its orbital flight.

"Something came by the right window," Lovell told the base. "It looked like a strap or a piece of paper. It struck the right window of the capsule and then bounced back. We never saw it again."

Borman and Lovell may have rammed or collided briefly with a bit of space junk: debris from exploded satellites or booster rockets. (Such a possibility is very, very remote, but it must not be ruled out.—F.E.) But what of the large object which Borman watched some distance from the Gemini? He is familiar with rockets and satellites and their components—but this was none of those. Before it vanished from the sight of the astronauts, it appeared to slow down and drop behind them. If that is the correct description of its maneuvers, then it was under some sort of intelligent control.

On June 4, 1965, Astronauts James McDivitt and Edward White were orbiting Earth, east of Hawaii. White was sleeping when McDivitt made pictures of a glowing, egg-shaped object which approached their capsule. McDivitt's description of the thing touched off a bit of a flap at the Space Center. At first he was told that it was the satellite Pegasus 2. That turned out to be a fantasy which had to be withdrawn, for Pegasus 2 was more than twelve hundred miles away at that time. Later the Pegasus 2 explanation was reinstated! The recheck, so we were told, had shown that the first figures were in error (by 1,200 miles?—F.E.) and that the thing was really Pegasus 2 after all! On August 18th, weeks after the event had transpired, Gemini Flight Director Chris Kraft issued still another public statement: "We think McDivitt probably saw a tank for one of the launch vehicles up there—probably one of our own."

If that incident did nothing else, it shows how excited the "experts" were when McDivitt described that glowing egg-shaped thing that was being photographed as it circled the Gemini capsule, leaving a contrail behind it from its propulsion system—a bit of evidence which is clearly visible in McDivitt's picture, which is reproduced in the picture section.

Astronauts John Young and Michael Collins had bettered the record by 3:24 a.m. on July 19, 1966. By that time they had traveled 476 miles into space, well beyond the Russian mark of 307 miles set by Cosmonauts Belyayev and Leonov sixteen months before. Collins and Young were literally "riding high" in Gemini 10. They had made six orbits of Earth and had traveled more than 150,000 miles in doing it; they had been farther from Earth than any other human beings and they were understandably exuberant.

Their enthusiasm changed to tones of wonderment when they suddenly discovered that they had company: two red glowing things ahead of them in space, evidently moving at the same speed in the same direction as the Gemini capsule.

"We've got two bright objects in our orbital path!" Young radioed down. "I don't think they are stars. We are going right along with them."

Ground control inquired:

"Where are the objects from you? If you can get a bearing maybe we can track them down."

A moment later Young radioed:

"They just disappeared! . . . I guess they were satellites of some kind."

It was later officially speculated that the objects might have been pieces of a Saturn rocket blown up in orbit during an unmanned flight early in July, 1966. In that case, it remains to be explained how the objects orbited along with the Gemini capsule and, if they were space junk, how they left that orbit and vanished so suddenly.

Friends of mine, who were present at the Space Center during this incident, tell me that the voice of Astronaut Young was cut off the intercom system for more than a minute as he began describing what he was watching. By the time he came back on the intercom he seemed to have been briefed, for that was when he "guessed" that he had only been seeing some satellite.

It would be understandable for the space officials to censor reports from astronauts, especially if they dealt with strange objects which might be UFOs. The reports from White and McDivitt had been embarrassing; the additional reports from Borman and Lovell added to the problem for the censors. By the time Young and Collins began reporting on the things they were watching, somebody's hand was on the switch, according to reports.

That censorship was included in the official policy was clearly established by October 12th when Julian Scheer, NASA's Assistant Administrator for Public Affairs, confirmed to the *New York Times* that a television camera *would* be aboard the planned fourteen-day orbital flight of an Apollo capsule.

Mr. Scheer told the *Times* that it was planned to send down television pictures from the first Apollo flight. Then he added:

"We want to show the American people whatever we can."

(Very considerate of them, since the American people put up every cent of the money to make the program possible.—F.E.)

Television had not been "required" in the Gemini flights, said this NASA spokesman . . . "but in the Apollo missions television becomes an operational aid. We can check on instruments and other things in the space crafts [Which, of course, the astronauts operating the camera could not do!—F.E.] and also look at the astronauts."

He added that an astronaut would also be able to hold the camera up to the window and focus on Earth below. This can also be done with a conventional movie camera or a still camera, with better detail and more lasting pictures.

Needless to say, but not mentioned in that interview, the astronauts could also turn their little hand-held television camera on any strange objects they encountered, such as "fragments of booster rockets" which showed an inclination to pace their capsule.

Says the *Times*:

"Just how frequently these pictures would be turned over to the networks has not been determined. Mr. Scheer said there was a possibility NASA might order a 5-second tape delay in releasing the pictures to the networks.

" 'We would like to exercise our ability to turn it off in certain cases,' he said. 'We need control in cases of emergency or matters of good taste. But it would not be censorship.' "

Continuing, the *Times* noted:

"In past space flights, NASA has frequently used the 5-second tape delay in releasing audio [radio.—F.E.] reports from the astronauts to the networks."

(See *New York Times*, October 12, 1966, front page and carry-over on page 25, Section L.)

Matters of good taste, the gentleman called it. NASA seems to be afraid those foul-talking astronauts might say a bad word . . . something like UFO, perhaps?

Let's take a look at the UFO development—in the rear-view mirror of time.

We have seen how closely the unfolding of the UFO problem has paralleled the first six phases of the space program as outlined at that briefing I attended in 1950. Year after year and step by step, the record reads like a replay of the program outlined to us that day so long ago. The approach; the study; the near-approach; the checking out of vehicles and attitudes; the surveillance; the display of the spacecraft to the greatest number of inhabitants to confirm presence and nonhostility.

257

It would seem reasonable to conclude that the mass sightings of 1965-1966-1967 were actually the Sixth Phase.

Millions of persons have reported seeing unconventional objects, according to a Gallup poll. A very large percentage of these sightings has taken place since the summer of 1965 and are still occurring at a record or near-record rate in mid-1967. Credible witnesses report near approaches and landings. From all over the world a veritable tide of UFO sightings is pouring in.

And perhaps most significantly, in space, where man is taking his first feeble steps toward venturing out into the solar system, and eventually beyond, UFOs have made their presence known.

Belatedly, our government has given indication of recognizing that the presence of the Unidentified Flying Objects is a *scientific* problem, and not a military problem.

This comes after several occasions where our astronauts have reported strange objects near their capsules—objects which did not fit into convenient categories for purposes of dismissal. Now we are told that future capsules will be equipped with television cameras—to record the experiences of the astronauts. And the television material, like the radio reports, will be subject to enough delay that they can admittedly be "edited"—should that seem advisable.

Is this part of the official program for dealing with an anticipated Phase Seven—what the military calls the "Overt Contact"?

Have the same high-placed policy makers who put the censorship order into effect in 1952 decided that ultimate contact with the UFOs is possibly imminent—or probably imminent?

Does it mean that we expect them to contact—or try to contact—one of our manned space capsules?

Is that why we have made arrangements to censor both the voice messages and the television broadcasts from the Apollo capsules—to enable those in power to control the content of the developments—to be released when and as they see fit?

The motives behind the procedures are a tightly guarded secret. It makes no sense to say that the astronauts are being subjected to a tape-delay "for reasons of good taste." The astronauts are gentlemen, every one. They are well-educated specialists, risking their lives in the service of their country—and of science. "Good taste?" They could give lessons on the subject!

To our way of reasoning, it would make good sense for the UFOs to contact our astronauts in orbit.

They would be contacting a well-educated, highly trained semi-official representative of a major power—under physical conditions which would be highly advantageous from the standpoint of the operators of the UFOs.

Contact with intelligent beings from another planet would have tremendous impact on the human race, theologically, psychologically, and sociologically.

If those in authority now conclude or suspect that contact with the UFOs is not far in the future, it behooves them to be extremely cautious about their approach to it. And if this is the real motive behind some of the programs and the policies which have baffled and bemused, perhaps there may be justification for them.

Contact, however it is made, would finally provide some long-awaited answers to this riddle—answers for which so many have waited for so long, and largely in vain.

Near Istanbul, Turkey, is Kandilli Observatory, where the astronomers were busy on August 23, 1966, making what they regarded as a routine study of solar flares. They were using a six-inch refracting telescope with a red filter over the lens.

They were startled to see a round black object moving across the field of view. Something spherical and solid was passing between the Observatory and the sun. No planet was in that position on that day, of course. The astronomers watched in wonderment during the short time it required for the object to cross the fiery disc of the sun.

Muammer Dizer, director of the solar work at Kandilli, reports that *seventeen minutes later another object followed the first, along the same path!* The puzzled astronomers took a photograph of the thing. This picture, published in *Sky and Telescope* magazine (Harvard Observatory) in February of 1967, shows a round black dot near the upper right center of the sun's disc. The magazine labeled the picture: "The Sun and an Artificial Satellite."

It was probably a logical assumption—but it proved to be an embarrassing guess.

Among the scientists who challenged the identification given to the object by the magazine was Victor Slabinski of Case Institute in Cleveland.

Since no planets or asteroids were between Earth and the sun on that day, and since *Sky and Telescope* had called the object an "artificial satellite," Mr. Slabinski went to the official records of satellite motion to determine just which two "artificial satellites" Kandilli might have seen.

The largest manmade satellite is Echo 2, which was neither large enough nor at the right position to have been the object in the Kandilli photograph, and in fact was not over Turkey at that time on that day.

The only Soviet satellites which were large enough were the Polyot and Proton 3. They had to be ruled out because

Polyot did not pass near Istanbul and Proton 3 was on the other side of Earth at the time of the sightings from Kandilli.

Other scientists pointed out that the object was not moving fast enough to have been an artificial satellite, as *Sky and Telescope* claimed. Others agreed with Mr. Slabinski that the object in the photograph was not large enough and still others noted that the shape of the image was inconsistent with the way a satellite would have photographed at the known shutter speed of 1/30 of a second.

The scientific evidence showed conclusively that the objects moving in tandem between Kandilli Observatory and the face of the sun were not any known natural objects, and could not have been artificial satellites.

That left but one hypothesis—that they were some form of Unidentified Flying Object—moving through space one behind the other, and much nearer to Earth than to the sun.

The first pictures ever made of UFOs were those taken by Professor Bonilla at the observatory in Zacatecas, Mexico, on August 12, 1883.

The most recent observatory pictures of a UFO were those taken by Kandilli Observatory and published in *Sky and Telescope* magazine for February, 1967.

Isn't this where we came in?